The Complete
Pyrography

The Complete Pyrography

Stephen Poole

Guild of Master Craftsman Publications Ltd

First published 1995 by
Guild of Master Craftsman
Publications Ltd,
166 High Street, Lewes,
East Sussex BN7 1XU

Text copyright © Stephen Poole 1995

Coyright in the Work © GMC Publications Ltd

Reprinted 1997, 1999, 2002, 2003, 2005

ISBN 0 946819 76 9

Front cover photograph by Zul Mukhida

Designed by Gellatly Norman Associates

Typefaces: Palatino and Franklin Gothic
demi bold

Origination by Viscan Graphics, Singapore

Printed by Kyodo Printing, Singapore

Dedication

To Tiny, my wife, and all our children,
John, Linsey, Vicky, Becky, Gary, Josh,
Bruce, Lucy and Sophie.

Important Note

Throughout this book, photocopies
of illustrations are recommended as
sources for pyrographed designs.
Unauthorized copying of copyright
material is illegal. You must always
check the copyright status of any
work you wish to copy and use.
**This is especially important if you
plan to try to sell your work.**

Check that the original work is
either not protected by copyright, or
apply to the copyright holder for
permission for its use.

Acknowledgements

Throughout a nearly twenty year period of producing, teaching and experimenting with pyrography, I have been privileged to make the acquaintance of a number of people without whom any progress in this craft would have been difficult, if not impossible. They are the following:

The late Eddie Chapleo who was the first person to convince me that my early work could be sold, and who kept us all amused on quiet days at the craft centre in East Bergholt with his impressions.

Copford Cricket Club from whom I obtained my first serious commission, a pyrograph of their pitch on a willow cricket bat (*see* below).

Essex journalist Liz Mullen who spotted the cricket bat and was subsequently instrumental in the planning and making of a television programme about the East Bergholt centre and the craftspeople working there.

Nan Taylor who opened a craft shop near the centre after our lease had expired and to this day has maintained an important outlet for local craftspeople.

Ron Bussey who provided me with free studio space at his printing works, thus allowing me to produce the larger framed works for an important exhibition demonstrating pyrography as an artform.

The Dedham Art Centre who provided the venue for the original two-day pyrography course.

Roy Child who first gave me the idea that a comprehensive guide to the art of pyrography was needed. He introduced me to my first hot-wire machine and has always gone out of his way to supply me with any equipment or research material from his company, Peter Child and Co.

Alex Woolf, my editor at GMC. My thanks for his interest in the subject, and his help in clarifying some of the more complicated explanations.

All the suppliers of pyrographic equipment and materials, in particular, Peter Child and Co., Janik Enterprises Ltd, and their MD John Faleur. Tony Palmby and his company, Copford Woodcraft Kitchens, who made me practically everything I wanted out of wood.

Finally, I would like to express my thanks to Tiny and our long-suffering family. For the last year the book has prevented me from carrying out many of the normal family functions. Fishing trips and picnics have played second fiddle to the typewriter and pyrography pencil. None of the family have ever complained, not even Tiny's mother Maria, who allowed me to use her flat to complete the work and kept up a constant supply of tea and bacon sandwiches throughout.

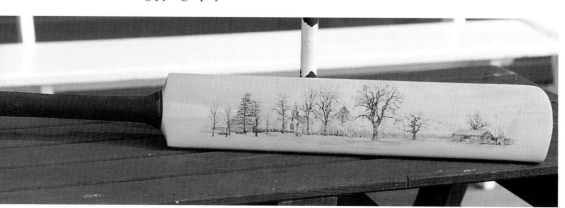

Contents

Introduction

'Pyrography', as any artist or hobbyist working in this medium will tell you, is rather an unfortunate word. Often confused with the manufacture of fireworks and acts of arson, the term was originally coined by the Victorians from the Greek words *pûr* (meaning 'fire') and *graphos* (meaning 'writing') to give a more grandiose title to the craft of pokerwork. To be fair, the term 'pokerwork' does tend to evoke images of identification marks being branded on tools and packing cases, and does little to stimulate interest in one of the oldest and most geographically widespread forms of wood decoration.

Pyrography has almost certainly been practised in one form or another since the discovery of fire itself. Primitive man must at some time have noticed the effect of using a stone or metal tool to scrape charred wood, forming a decoration from the uncharred wood beneath the surface.

Pyrography, as our ancestors understood it, was an artistic craft. It was very popular in Europe during the 17th century when it was used principally for decorating small items of woodware. Much of the work was similar in style to the designs found in contemporary silverware and needlework. Later it became fashionable to decorate furniture with pyrographic panels, although much of this work was imported from the east.

During the 19th century, pyrographers achieved a very high standard of craftsmanship. However, it remained no more than a pastime for them, probably because the basic nature of their tools prevented them from working at a commercially viable speed. A typical early-Victorian pyrography tool kit would have comprised a portable charcoal pot or stove perforated all the way round near the top by a series of holes into which pointed pokers with varying shaped ends were inserted for heating in the hot charcoal. Asbestos yarn would have been wrapped around the handles of the pokers which, when they had been heated for any length of time, would become uncomfortable to hold.

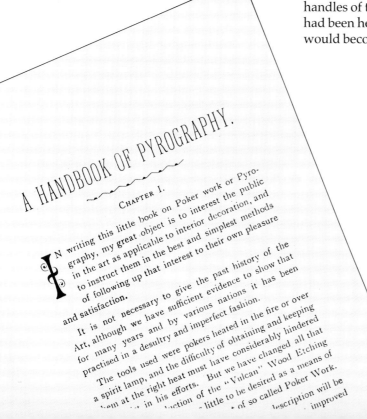

The opening page from Mrs M. Maude's *A Handbook of Pyrography*.

An advertisement for pyrography lessons appearing in Mrs Maude's book.

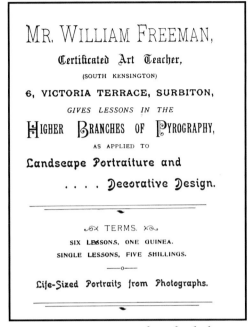

MR. WILLIAM FREEMAN,

Certificated Art Teacher,

(SOUTH KENSINGTON)

6, VICTORIA TERRACE, SURBITON,

GIVES LESSONS IN THE

HIGHER BRANCHES OF PYROGRAPHY,

AS APPLIED TO

Landscape Portraiture and

. . . . Decorative Design.

✳ TERMS. ✳

SIX LESSONS, ONE GUINEA.

SINGLE LESSONS, FIVE SHILLINGS.

Life-Sized Portraits from Photographs.

It is quite remarkable how high the standard of some of the work was when one takes into account the problems of inconsistent heat that were experienced. On a larger-scale piece of work it would have been necessary to have an assistant passing pokers back and forth, and care would have had to be taken to work on deeply engraved areas while the poker was 'fresh', moving to more delicate parts of the design when the poker had cooled. Much of this work has survived and can be seen in the Pinto collection stored at the City of Birmingham Museum. Towards the end of the Victorian era, gas and electric stoves and furnaces were introduced along with platinum-tipped pokers. These went some way towards easing the problem of inconsistent heat.

The poker was not the only means by which Victorian pyrographers could make their mark. Blow pipes were available making it possible to produce wash and tint effects. The most famous of these was probably the 'Vulcan burnt wood etching machine'. I cannot claim to have personally seen one of these machines, but a book entitled *A Handbook of Pyrography* by a Mrs M. Maude, which appeared in 1891, was effectively an advertisement for the machine (*see* left). The book contains much of interest for those wishing to learn more about Victorian pokerwork; many pages are devoted to advertising wooden blanks available in timbers still popular today. Also advertised are the services of pyrography tutors, showing how popular the craft was (*see* left). The most astonishing part of the book for me was the Vulcan machine itself (*see* page 4). The apparatus had the appearance of a large scent spray bottle to which was fitted a length of rubber tubing and a pair of bellows. The bottle was filled with benzolene, petrol or spirit, which was then pumped by the bellows and ignited through a platinum point at the end of the rubber tube. There was a selection of different types of point, and these could be part exchanged for new ones when worn out. It was also recommended that a small container of nitric acid was placed close by for removing pieces of charred matter from the end of the point as they built up. I would have dearly liked to try one of these machines for myself, though I cannot help but think of them as little more than petrol bombs and not the sort of thing to have on the kitchen table. Modern electric pyrography tools are, by contrast, extremely safe.

In the early part of this century, a soldering-iron type of pyrography tool was developed (*see* page 16 for a full description). This was a great improvement on the Victorian equipment, and is still used by many pyrographers, but is is nevertheless unwieldy and becomes quite hot to handle when used for any length of time.

In 1962, Roy Child, son of the late woodturning expert, Peter Child, had a go at improving one such machine. Roy, then aged 15 and interested in all things electrical, designed a pen for the existing transformer that all but eliminated the aforementioned disadvantages. By 1973 Peter Child 'hot-wire' pyrography machines were in full production, now much improved with stainless steel terminals and a specially designed pen that minimized the heating of the handle.

The Janik 'solid-point' machine was

launched in 1975. Although not as versatile as the Peter Child hot-wire machine, its ease of use and relative inexpensiveness meant that it rapidly established itself as the market leader in the field. The two types of machine are in many ways complementary, and today's pyrographers often use them both side by side. (Janik now also make a hot-wire machine.)

Despite these modern advances, primitive techniques are still used to pyrographically decorate wood and other materials (*see* pages 5 and 6). In Madagascar, for example, whole surface areas are burned with a red-hot metal 'spade'. The artist then removes with a knife or scissors a thin layer of the charred wood, exposing the original colour and thus creating a design that stands out in contrast.

In Peru it is still possible to see llamas carrying calabashes decorated with pyrography travelling on the same roads now used by modern lorries, demonstrating the survival in today's society of this old and popular craft.

Pyrography has always been used as a means of decorating eating utensils. There can hardly be a country in Central Europe, Africa or South America without examples of this kind of work (*see* page 7). The Museum of Mankind in Paris boasts a wonderful collection of such objects from around the world.

It is clear that anything metal that can be heated directly in the fire can be used as a pyrography tool. However, this book will cover only those techniques that offer the best possible results using the modern hot-wire and solid-point machines.

Pyrography as a craft or art form is available to anyone wishing to have a go and there is no need to have had a formal art training, or to be a practising professional or amateur. Many of the students who have participated in my courses were talked into taking part after

An advertisement for the Vulcan machine which is described at length in *A Handbook of Pyrography.*

protesting that the nearest they had come to being creative was doodling on a telephone directory. They were quite surprised by how quickly they grasped the techniques, and many went on to produce some excellent work.

When practised purely as a hobby, pyrography certainly has a therapeutic value for those needing to relax and take their minds off the pressures of everyday life. For those who succeed in attaining any sort of standard in their work – and as the author of this book I must optimistically say that means everybody – it can be a way of supplementing your income. At the very least you will be able to sell pieces of your work to family and friends to pay for supplies of blanks.

None of the equipment used in pyrography is sophisticated, costly or difficult to use. If you are able to sit at a table and coordinate one good eye with one good arm, you can do it!

Many of the projects in this book have a wildlife theme. My interest in nature has inclined me towards this type of illustration, and I find that the best way to pass on my own discoveries is through such projects. However, readers of this book should not feel they must restrict their subject matter to examples of flora and fauna. While there is no doubt that many wildlife subjects lend themselves to the medium of pyrography, with its facility for producing textures and effects similar to those found in nature, it doesn't

The pieces shown below and on page 6 were created by a gentleman in Norfolk who used heated pieces of metal to good crude effect.

have to end there. The skills you will learn by reading this book will enable you to produce any kind of work you want. If you intention is to produce cartoons, or little designs on wooden plaques such as those hung on children's bedroom doors, you will be able to enliven such pyrographs no end by following the advice and examples in this book. The exercises included here are purely a means of teaching people how to obtain the widest range of effects and the most interesting textures and tones from what is essentially a piece of heated metal.

As can be seen on the pages of this Introduction, amazing things can be achieved in pyrography using the most simple of tools. Bear in mind, however, that the hot-wire machine, by its very nature, is much more versatile than the other major tool available – the solid-point machine. I used an original Peter Child hot-wire machine to complete all the projects in this book, with the exception of the sampler on pages 44 to 50, and the bowl in Chapter 12.

Nevertheless, it is perfectly possible to attempt all the projects, except for the advanced work in Chapter 13, using the solid-point machine or any other woodburning equipment for that matter, although the results will almost inevitably be rather less subtle than those seen in the photographs. If you are using the Janik G4 solid-point machine, the best points to use for the projects in this book, are the B21, which has a surface area closest in size to a hot-wire standard point, and the B24, which is equivalent to the hot-wire spoon point. If you are not using Janik or Peter Child equipment, you need to use a heated round-ended point similar in size to the tip of the average ball-point pen.

Pyrographed items acquired on a trip to southern Turkey in 1988.

CHAPTER 1

Materials

Although pyrography can be applied to virtually any surface that can be burned or charred, e.g. leather, bone, cork, etc., I have found that wood offers the best results both in variety of texture and practicability. Wood has the added advantage of being a raw material that can be either turned on a lathe or carved into a multitude of shapes and objects.

■ What kind of wood?

There are well over 50,000 species of tree known to man. These can be divided into two main categories: softwood conifers and deciduous hardwoods. The former are used in the main for the manufacture of paper and chipboard, while the latter are of more interest to the carpenter, woodturner and indeed the pyrographer.

Let us consider the ideal properties required for pyrography on a wood surface. A light colour will show your work at its best, bringing out more of the detail and fine textures. However, not all light-coloured woods are suitable, since some are very grainy. Pine, for example, is cheap to buy and it burns well, but the difference in texture between the grain and the actual 'meat' of the wood is so great that it is difficult to burn a continuous line when passing the wire or point through the grain. Some people are able to use pine and other grainy woods to good effect; however they tend to restrict one to subjects that require a minimum of detail.

Another example of wood unsuited to pyrography is unfortunately oak. Although oak has a light colour, and is one of the most durable woods, its grain is so hard that it almost refuses to burn altogether. However, please do not be discouraged from trying these awkward woods.

Sycamore

From my own experience, sycamore has to be at the top of the list of ideal woods (*see* Fig 1.1). Sycamore has traditionally been used in the manufacture of kitchen utensils, e.g. wooden spoons, spatulas, breadboards, chopping boards etc. The large chopping block tables seen in butchers shops and restaurant kitchens are all made from sycamore. Unlike some woods, such as pine, sycamore has no characteristic odour or taste and the surface is certainly more friendly to the sharpened cutting edge of an expensive knife. By a happy coincidence, it is also an ideal wood for pyrography. This is partly because of its light colour, but mainly because of the extremely small difference in hardness between the grain parts and the non-grain parts, which makes it relatively easy to pyrograph.

In addition to sycamore, there are a number of other similar woods, such as horse chestnut, holly, boxwood, lime and English or Canadian maple (closely related to sycamore) that are exceptionally useful to the pyrographer. There is also another material that I have used in vast quantities, and I strongly recommend that you find a source for this early on: this is birch-faced plywood.

Birch-faced plywood

This material is not likely to be found at your local DIY store. However, it can be obtained from the larger trade suppliers

Fig 1.1
Various sycamore blanks.

in 8ft x 4ft (2.44m x 1.22m) sheets. Always ask for offcuts; if you have to buy a complete sheet the supplier will normally be able to cut it down into more manageable pieces. I have come across birch-faced ply at the premises of specialist kitchen manufacturers and die makers; perhaps you are fortunate enough to have one of these in your area. Such places inevitably accumulate waste material that they are unable to use.

Birch-faced ply is identical to sycamore in appearance, and when sanded will give a very smooth, white surface to pyrograph on (*see* Fig 1.2). The grain reacts to the pyrography tool in almost exactly the same way as the rest of the wood. The only real differences between sycamore and birch-faced ply are that the ply is softer and cheaper. Thus it is no good for certain pyrography blanks (i.e. objects prepared for pyrography); a spoon, for example, would quickly fall apart, yet it is ideal for a flat illustration. A picture or design on a thin gauge of birch-faced ply can be framed in the conventional way.

Because of its similarity to sycamore, it is always useful to have a scrap with you when working as a means of testing for the correct temperature etc. directly before you apply the tool to the actual wood you are working on. If your workplace is a good table in the house, you can keep a sheet of ply cut to fit the work area you are using.

Veneers

A veneer is a controlled shaving from a piece of prepared wood (*see* Fig 1.3). Using veneers is an inexpensive way to experiment with a wide variety of wood surfaces. A veneer can be adhered to hardboard or cheap plywood by using a contact adhesive, giving you a more solid work area. Decorative veneers are usually approximately 0.6mm ($\frac{1}{42}$in) thick and have been used by carpenters and cabinetmakers for centuries.

The larger veneer suppliers will normally stock up to 100 different woods in veneer form. A lot of these are not going to be suitable for pyrography purposes, but for a small sum you can buy a veneer collector's set containing 50 types of wood, all labelled with basic information including trade and botanical names, common names and country of origin. A discussion of some of the

veneers available follows:

Yew

This is a very hard wood, but that need not necessarily be a disadvantage. You will find that, although its hardness means that it takes longer to make marks, it does enable you to produce more detailed work. Most yew is rather dark, but there are areas of much lighter wood found nearer the bark. It is a wood that turns very well on a lathe, and has a beautiful, smooth touch when sanded. When buying full sheets of veneer, you can study them for the more interesting markings and choose the one you want.

Horse chestnut

Similar in colour to sycamore and with a less pronounced grain, horse chestnut would be a good choice for an illustration where little interference from grain markings is desired. It is a little softer than sycamore, but its softness can help in the forming of deeper grooves for texturing.

Bird's-eye maple

Imagine a sandy beach where the tide has completely ebbed; the sand has been formed in ripples by the receding waves, and pebbles, shells and small stones have been left embedded in the wet sand. Well, you could be just as easily looking at a piece of bird's-eye maple. I have seen

pieces so beautifully marked that they should have been framed and exhibited just as they were. The surface pyrographs well, though you have to avoid the larger 'pebble' markings with the pyrography tool as they have a tendency to burn in a different and inconsistent way.

Pear

This is normally a reasonably dark wood, but it sands to a very smooth finish. Like horse chestnut, the grain markings offer very little resistance to the pyrography tool, however your work will have to be more heavily burned to give you the contrast you need against the darkness of the wood.

It is worth noting that the above descriptions of how these woods behave are based on my experiences with specific pieces of material. No two pieces of wood are ever identical; you will gain the best experience by trying the various woods yourself.

Fig 1.2 (above left)
Birch-faced ply.
Fig 1.3 (above)
A selection of veneers.

◼ Using grain markings and blemishes

Unlike the pages of a sketch pad, wood surfaces vary a great deal – even pieces cut from the same sheet of plywood. However, you will often be able to put to good use the natural grain markings of woods such as sycamore, maple and birch. Even large knots and other imperfections can usually, with a little imagination, be incorporated into your work. I have had a great deal of success with wildlife illustrations, and many times have been glad of a natural marking that could be made to look like a twig or branch for example.

Similarly there have been occasions when a particularly interesting blemish has inspired and helped to compose an entire picture. I can well remember a scrap piece of oak that came into my possession one day. After a good sanding and cleaning, the various imperfections and grain lines began to take on the appearance of coastal mud flats. Of the entire surface of the wood, only a small section in the corner was free from any markings, and in this area I pyrographed a small old wooden rowing boat that looked abandoned and unlikely to float on the incoming tide. The pyrography only took an hour.
The oak tree had

composed the rest of the picture for me over a period of several hundred years.

◼ Where else can you find material to pyrograph?

Apart from the recognized suppliers of blanks, there are other sources that you can explore. Kitchen reject shops have become very popular in recent years. The advantage of obtaining blanks from this kind of source is cost. You would have to pay around three times as much for a handmade breadboard in English kiln-dried sycamore, as you would for a breadboard in beech from a reject shop. You will not need to be reminded, of course, that you get what you pay for.

Kitchen reject shops usually have a section displaying a large number of wooden items. Most of these are mass produced from beech (*see* Fig 1.4). These breadboards, chopping boards, spoons, egg cups etc. have not been made intentionally for pyrographers, but you can sift through many similarly made pieces to find the ones with the best surface.

Beech is considerably harder than

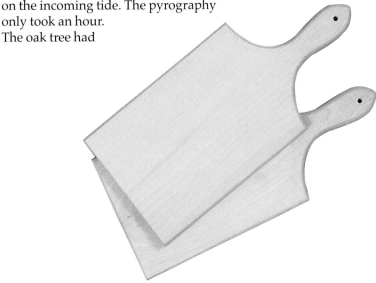

Fig 1.4
Beech cheese boards.

sycamore; it is a darker wood, with a slightly pinkish hue. Although these objects are made in large quantities, they are usually made quite well. Remember, however, that if a piece is made from three or more separate pieces of timber, unless you know what wood adhesive has been used, it is best not to burn through any of these joints.

You may be lucky enough to know of a local hobbyist woodturner, in which case it may be worth approaching them with an offer to buy blanks. I have been very lucky over the years with the various craft fairs I have participated in. I have met many excellent turners who are prepared, for a fee, to supply me with quantities of such things as thimbles, rolling pins, napkin rings and egg cups. There are also professional woodturners working for specialist kitchen-unit and furniture manufacturers who could produce items for you.

Always be on the lookout for suitable and interesting pieces of wood. You never know where they might turn up. Keep a watchful eye open at boot sales for old wooden items such as boxes and pieces of turned wood. Even if they are varnished or painted they can often be rubbed down and used as one-off items for pyrography work. Scraps of wood washed up on the tide, having been smoothed by the action of the sea and bleached by the sun, can also be the basis for interesting pieces of work. Never leave the workplace of a woodturner or woodworker without checking the scrap bin!

CHAPTER 2

Sources for Composition

I am continually on the lookout for reference material for compositions, particularly if a request has been made for a specific subject. There are various places where you can look for such material with a view to creating your own reference library. (Before reading this chapter please refer to the note on page v concerning copyright.)

▮ Places to look

You may have some old books and magazines that are no longer needed. Check through them for anything that might be useful in the future. Make sure that you don't restrict your selection to subjects that catch your eye because you like them for other reasons. Recently, I was scanning through an old trade printing journal when I came across an advert for a printing product that featured a seascape, complete with sailing ships. The ships I had no immediate interest in, but a small seagull in the top right-hand corner was precisely what I needed for a composition where I was struggling a bit. Had I not studied the whole advert, I would have missed it.

Libraries are

an obvious source, especially for those wishing to locate composition material for subjects they wish to specialize in. Jumble sales were also once an excellent source of cheap books and magazines, although they seem to have become a part of our history. However, the old-fashioned jumble sale has been replaced by the giant boot sale, one of the best hunting grounds ever. You may even be lucky enough to find old craft magazines and books dating back to Victorian times and the early decades of the twentieth century. If you are able to get your hands on any copies of Weldon's 'Sixpenny Series' magazine (*see* Fig 2.2), for example, you will find that many interesting crafts are covered, usually accompanied by highly adaptable

Fig 2.1
A floral design taken from a 1930s craft magazine. It was a design intended for leather engraving the flap of a handbag.

illustrations and plans.

A well-meaning great aunt once gave me an old book that she thought I might find useful. The book lacked any reference to pyrography in the contents pages, and was subsequently shelved. Several years later, being somewhat wiser, I studied it more carefully. A chapter devoted to metalwork and, in particular, the manufacture of ornamental box-lid hinges, provided the inspiration for the shading project in this book (*see* Chapter 10).

■ The importance of photocopying

I remember well one of the first pieces of work I completed and sold. In those early days I struggled with a very basic soldering-iron-type pyrography tool loaned to me by a friend. I had seen a picture in an old cookery book of a lobster. Having acquired earlier some

rather superb large sycamore chopping boards, I proceeded to sketch the lobster onto the wood. It was far more complicated than I had at first thought, and took over an hour to complete the sketch / plan. I was very impressed with my pyrographic efforts; the lobster took around four hours to complete and was sold quite quickly from a display of my work in a local public house.

Having spent so much time on the piece, using a tool more suited to burning house signs, I was not overenthusiastic about repeating the same lobster a few days later when a request was made for another one. I decided this time to photocopy the original from the book and

Fig 2.2
Weldon's 'Sixpenny Series' magazines – a useful source of designs and illustrations for pyrography.

trace the lobster straight onto the board. The photocopy lost a lot of the fine detail, but the basics were all there, and I was able to trace the main parts onto the wood in a matter of minutes, adding what I needed of the fine detail directly onto the wood afterwards. I realized the wisdom of what I had done some time later when a third request for a lobster on a chopping board was ordered after I had returned the loaned cookery book. I still had my photocopy which could be used many times.

The moral of the above story is that it is always worth photocopying designs or illustrations that you have used or think you might use in the future. This is not only because you might mislay the original; if you trace directly through the original enough times it will soon become unusable and possibly difficult to replace. To save costs you can photocopy a few items at a time by cutting up the images and pasting them down onto an A4 sheet to make one copy that can be broken up later.

All photocopying results in some loss of detail, particularly when copying colour photographs or prints. Therefore, if you can, you should keep the original and attach it to the photocopy. You will find after using the photocopy-tracing method for a little while, that this loss of detail actually helps you. A bad photocopy can be a good plan to work from, alleviating the need to trace in too much of the fine detail which can be added later anyway.

Most libraries have their own photocopying facilities, which can be useful if you plan to use their reference sections for source material.

Before copying anything, always check with the librarian that you are not infringing any copyright.

▪ Creating a reference library

My experience with the lobster

pyrograph led to my first filed references, and since then any interesting subject material has been photocopied and filed for future use. Unless you want to spend time looking in libraries, bookshops and stationers every time you are called upon to produce a specific pyrographed subject, it is worth starting such a collection straight away. Magazine cuttings and photocopies can be stored in an inexpensive expanding filing wallet – the bigger the better.

I have built up a separate reference library over the years of my own photography. If I am commissioned to produce a pyrograph of a building or scene, whenever possible I like to work from my own pictures. I am particularly interested in photographing wildlife, and I own a good camera with standard and macro lenses, which is ideal for this purpose. I have shot many wildlife action poses with this camera; I have even managed to use – and this may sound a little macabre – some of the bank voles, field mice and other small mammals that have died at the claws of a cat that lives near my old studio on a farm in Essex. They were brought to life with the help of some pins, wire and glue for their final photocall.

▪ Conclusion

You just do not know where you will find the ideal source for your next composition, which is why you should never throw away anything that might contain a useful pictorial reference without checking it first. Clearly there is no shortage of material, and if you collect, organize and file it properly you might just have to hand what you need when you need it. Never pass a car boot sale if you see one without taking a look, and locate your nearest photocopying facility. I hope my suggestions and my own experiences inspire you to create a comprehensive library of reference material for yourselves.

CHAPTER 3

Tools and Equipment

This chapter provides a comprehensive list, including detailed descriptions, of the equipment, tools and accessories required in order to embark on pyrography.

■ Pyrography equipment

There are various pyrography tools available from craft supply shops and mail order catalogues, and they can be divided into the following three types.

Soldering-iron type

Usually German or British manufactured, this tool is inexpensive and limited in its uses. It works on the same principle as the soldering iron, the working point being heated by a cylindrical element or coil contained in the working end of the tool. A variety of interchangeable points can be

Fig 3.1
The Janik G4 solid-point pyrography machine.

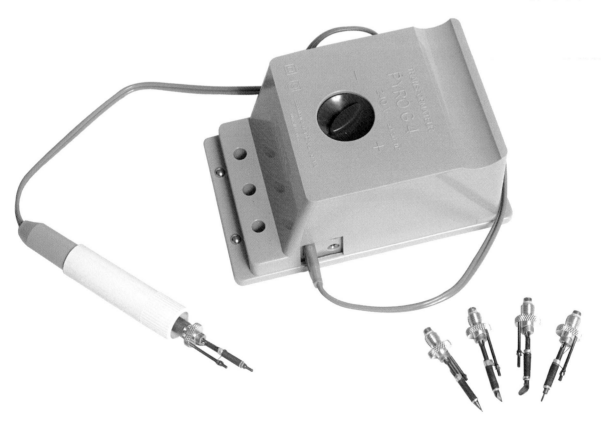

Fig 3.2
The Janik G4HW hot-wire
pyrography machine.

fitted into the holder and secured by a
screw. The disadvantages are that the
whole thing soon becomes very hot and
uncomfortable to handle and, with the
expansion of the hot metal, the points are
difficult to keep in place; worst of all, you
have no real facility for adjusting the
temperature of the point. This was my
first pyrography tool, and I am grateful
for it, if only because it stirred my
enthusiasm.

Solid-point type

This type of equipment uses solid
working points, each of which is
provided with its own miniature heating
element close to the tip. In terms of
numbers sold this machine remains by far
the most popular type of pyrography
tool.

The solid-point machines represent a
substantial progression from the
soldering-iron machines. A good
selection of points is available in all
shapes and sizes, as well as brands.

This type of equipment offers most to
the pyrographer wishing to specialize in
bold pattern and repeat pattern designs.
The flat-ended points are extremely
efficient when large areas of uniform
shading are needed. Likewise, when a
considerable area of black, or a very
heavily burnt area is required, for a house
sign for instance, the solid-point machine
is the quickest and most effective tool for
the job.

Brands are a useful kind of decorating
tool, particularly for the less confident
draughtsman. Most of the available
brands produce variations on a few
basic shapes – mainly circles, triangles

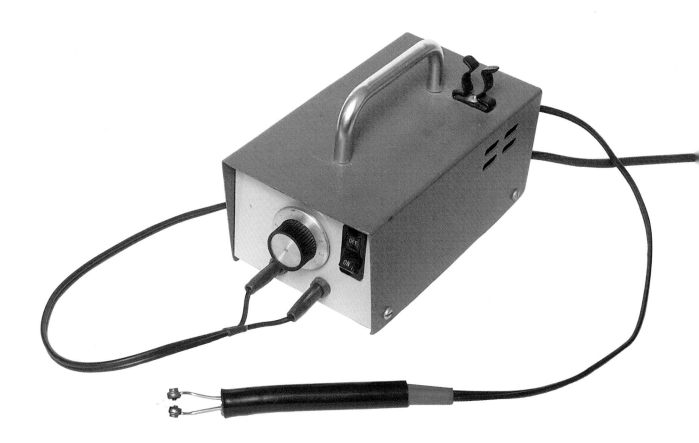

Fig 3.3
The Peter Child hot-wire pyrography machine.

and squares, and it is surprising how much design scope there is when they are used imaginatively. Designs can be planned and laid out by dipping the brand in an ordinary rubber stamp ink pad and printing it out on a sheet of paper.

This is a fun piece of equipment and I wonder, had I found this model before discovering the hot-wire machines, whether my work would have developed in a completely different way.

Hot-wire type

This type of tool does not have a *solid* working point, but a flexible point or nib made from a short length of nickel chromium wire and held between two terminals fitted to the end of a pencil or holder (*see* Fig 3.2). The working voltage of the hot-wire tool can be much lower than the soldering-iron type, and the heat of the point is capable of fine adjustment through a control box. In my opinion it is the best of the equipment available and for those who wish to gain the maximum benefit from the instructional chapters of this book, it is the machine I would recommend.

Both Peter Child & Co. and Janik make hot-wire machines, and all of the projects in this book are possible with either machine.

All the work I do is carried out with either a standard wire point or a spoon point. Spoon points are simply wire points shaped at the very end into a spoon shape by the application of a sharp blow with a tiny round steel punch (*see* page 23). It is also possible to make your own brands shaped from wire for decorative and repeat patterns.

Fig 3.4
Tools required by users of hot-wire pyrography machines, including hammer, screwdrivers, pliers, nickel chromium wire and wire cutters.

■ Tools specifically for users of hot-wire pyrography machines

Pliers

These are very important for use in the manufacture of wire points, or for adapting the points for different kinds of work with a hot-wire machine (*see* page 23).

Small anvil

You could go out and actually buy a small anvil, but an old large hammer head or lump hammer head will suffice.

Wire cutters

These are for accurately cutting lengths of wire for use as points (*see* page 22).

Small screwdriver

This is for loosening and tightening the screws and clamps holding the points in place on hot-wire machines (*see* page 23).

■ General accessories

Angle-poise lamp

Whether you are fortunate enough to have a naturally lit, purpose-built studio, or you are currently using the end of the kitchen table, you will need an angle-poise lamp in order to see clearly what you are doing. Working with a lamp set at a slight angle to the surface will highlight the tiny shadows formed in the grooves of the pyrograph.

Pencils

You will need a small selection of both hard and soft pencils. B or 2B is recommended for the soft pencil work, which involves sketching or drawing on to a wood surface. There will always be lines in your sketch that are not covered by the pyrography and these will have to be erased with a soft rubber or, if necessary, sandpapered away. The reason why soft pencils are used is because hard pencils will often leave a detectable indentation in the wood.

For all tracing, use a hard pencil – the harder the better. 2H up to 4H is recommended. The main reason for this is that a finely sharpened, hard pencil will stay sharp for a long time and will give a continuous fine trace line.

Pencil sharpener and scalpel

When buying a pencil sharpener it is worth buying a good one, and the sharpeners cast in metal are the best.

Scalpels can be obtained from various suppliers to the hobby trade, model shops or printers' suppliers. The blade to ask for is the 10A, which will fit the No. 3 scalpel handle. The 10A blade has a fine point and, as you would expect with a blade designed for a surgeon, it is very sharp.

Scalpels are used as a means of removing minor errors. It can be heartbreaking to make a small mistake with a detail in pyrography – a line continued a touch too far, a highlight in an eye burnt in by mistake. Quite often these mistakes can be rectified by carefully scraping away the offending mark with the point of a scalpel blade.

Soft rubber

A soft white rubber is an essential part of the pyrographer's tool kit. It is used to remove any surplus marks and lines from the initial plan that has been pencil drawn on to the wood. Alternatively, a putty rubber can be applied to black or pencil carbon marks in cases where a mark has been made too heavily and requires toning down, but not outright removal.

Brown masking tape

This is used for adhering photocopies or design plans to the wood surface. Masking tape is preferred to Sellotape because it is less likely to leave any gum marks or stains on the wood. Used extensively in the reprographic and paint-spraying trades, it is available at most garages and office suppliers.

Black pencil carbon paper

This may pose a problem. The best pencil

Fig 3.5
General accessories for the pyrographer. These include a scalpel, black pencil carbon paper, fine sandpaper, a soft rubber, pencils, sable brushes, masking tape and an angle-poise lamp.

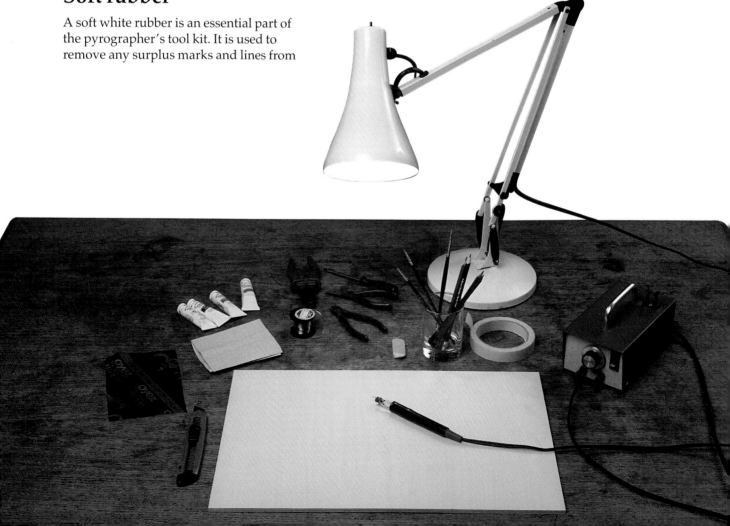

carbon paper for the pyrographer's purposes is a type once commonly used in the legal profession for making true copies of documents. One A4 sheet could be used for six months continuously and still have plenty of carbon left in it. However, with the advent of electronic and computer technology, it has since become quite rare. It is still made, but you may have to hunt for it. If you cannot find this particular product, you may have to resort to a black *ink* carbon paper. Never use blue carbon – it is virtually impossible to remove all the trace lines with burning, and when work is completed, it will invariably have a faint blue tint.

Steel ruler

You will have a lot of use for a ruler. A steel ruler is particularly useful if you have to pyrograph an accurate straight line. Using an ordinary point, you can steer it along the ruler on a fairly low temperature setting to make a groove that can then be easily followed with a hotter point.

Plastic set square or small T-square

These are highly useful for centring designs on to a surface.

Sandpaper

This is needed primarily for smoothing the wood surface before beginning, although good-quality blanks are often smooth enough to work on without sanding. However, I always make it a rule to sand the wood with *fine* sandpaper

before commencing the tracing or pyrography, because this ensures that the surface has been studied. A fine paper will not rough the surface, and it is often at this point that grain markings and imperfections are noticed that determine vital decisions such as which way up on the wood and in what precise position the design should be placed. So, always sand the wood.

A handy item to accompany the

Fig 3.6 (right)
Sable brushes.

sandpaper is a piece of corduroy, which is perfect for wiping off any remaining particles of sanded wood that cannot be removed by blowing or brushing.

Sable brushes

If you intend to add colour to your pyrography, you will need a small selection of brushes. Sable brushes are expensive, but unfortunately there is no real substitute (*see* Fig 3.6). Two or three from size 0 upwards would be enough. You will probably only use water-based paints, so they will be easy to clean and last a very long time.

CHAPTER 4

Constructing Wire Points

To be used to its best advantage, the hot-wire pyrography tool must be considered an engraving tool as much as anything else, and the advantage it has over pencil, charcoal, watercolour brush, etc., is its ability to alter the surface to which it is applied, making it possible to produce an endless variety of textures and tones. In many cases it is possible to suggest the texture of the subject and give an additional three-dimensional quality to the pyrograph.

Constructing a standard wire point

In order to produce these effects the making of a correct wire point is of paramount importance, and it is worth taking a detailed look at the best way to do this. There are four grades of Nichrome wire for making points: 26SWG (finest), 25SWG, 24SWG and 23SWG (thickest). These are obtainable from specialist suppliers. It can be argued that one gauge is marginally better than another for certain types of work or for making shaped points or brands for more specific uses. Generally speaking, however, everything can be done with one gauge, and the best one to use is 24SWG.

Fig 4.1
With a pair of pliers or wire cutters, cut a piece of 24SWG wire, approximately ¾in (19mm) long.

Fig 4.2
Using the ball of your forefinger and thumb . . .

Fig 4.3
. . . bend it into a U-shape.

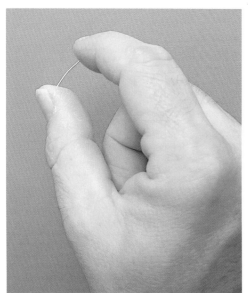

Fig 4.1

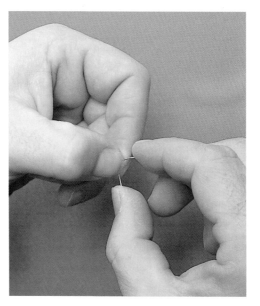

Fig 4.2

Fig 4.3

Fig 4.4
Loosen the screws sufficiently to allow the ends of the wires to slide between the prongs and the retaining grommets. Then retighten, being careful to avoid bending the prongs together. To produce a good range of marks and textures, you will need to exert a fair amount of pressure on the point, and the shorter the point the less likely it is to bend. Makers' recommendations vary, but in my own experience I have found a point length of ⅜in (10mm), once tightened into position, produces very good results.

Fig 4.5
With a pair of pliers, pinch the loop approximately halfway down to form a secondary loop.

Fig 4.6
As near to the end of the secondary loop as possible, pinch the wire completely together.

Fig 4.7
Finally, gently bend the point with the pliers until it slopes at a comfortable angle to the work surface.

Fig 4.8 (below)
A spoon point.

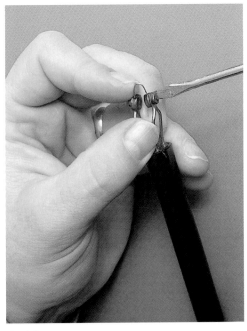

Fig 4.4

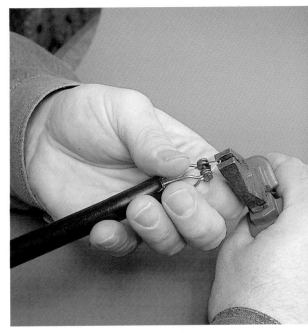

Fig 4.5

Fig 4.6

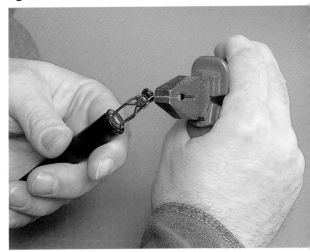

Fig 4.7

▪ Constructing other kinds of point

Ready-made spoon points can be bought (*see* Fig 4.8). They can also be made quite easily by taking a standard wire point and hammering it out flat on a hard metal anvil such as the head of a hammer held in a vice. Any sharp edges can be removed by rubbing on abrasive paper.

If you have a hot-wire machine but still need to burn deep, dark areas for house signs, or to produce brands for decorative and repeat patterns, it is possible to make your own brands out of nickel chromium wire. Heavy gauge wire, such as 24 or 23SWG, is needed for rigidity. The brands are formed using small pointed pliers. Accuracy is important here so that the whole of the pattern surface touches evenly in use. The pencil is usually held in a vertical position for branding.

CHAPTER 5

Starting Out

Before you actually put pen to wood, so to speak, there are a number of factors which need to be addressed. These include safety, surface preparation, lighting, and setting the temperature of the point.

■ Safety

Modern pyrography is a very safe activity if carried out responsibly, and a lot of the potential hazards can be avoided by the use of common sense. However, there are a few safety measures that should be borne in mind before you begin to use your pyrography equipment. The following is a summary of the safety precautions applicable to most types of pyrography machine:

■ Do not open the case of the power unit. Live terminals are exposed inside. Do not attempt to service the power unit without expert knowledge. Do not allow children to poke anything into the ventilation slots in the case.

■ The fumes from burning wood can be unpleasant at times but are rarely dangerous. However, regular pyrographers are advised to use a fan. Fans with carbon filters for removing smell and smoke are available.

■ Avoid twisting and bending the flex at the end of the pencil or the strands of wire inside the insulation will eventually break. Do not wind the flex around the handle when storing the pencil.

■ Do not use the control unit to power any other appliance. It has a very low voltage AC output. The pencil will not work on 12 volts or any other transformer.

■ The front panel may get hot in use. This is quite normal and depends on the heat control setting.

■ Protect the unit from damp and rain.

Safety for hot-wire users

■ Do not let the pencil terminals touch together, short out against a metal object, or touch the case of the control unit. There is a risk of permanent damage to the control unit if it is subjected to short circuits for more than a minute or so.

■ NEVER let the hot point anywhere near the mains cable as it could quickly burn through. If you let children use the machine, make sure they keep the cable clear of the work area.

■ The points get very hot and could potentially start a fire. Stow the pencil in the clip on the power unit instead of putting it down on the bench. Supervise young or irresponsible users. Do not leave the machine unattended and switch off after use.

■ The wires used to make the point must not be too short. Different machines have different attachments; always follow manufacturers' recommendations concerning the length of the wires. In my experience, a finished point ⅜in (10mm) from the terminal gives excellent results.

■ Avoid bending the terminal support struts which are of necessarily delicate design in order to reduce heat flow to the handle.

■ From time to time, you may need to dismantle the pencil terminals and clean off tarry deposits to cure bad contacts. Oven cleaner is ideal for this and will not attack stainless steel. However, do not let the oven cleaner touch the handle or get inside the pen.

Preparing the surface of the wood

Good quality birch-faced plywood and prepared blanks do not usually need sanding further. However, I have always encouraged my students to gently sandpaper the surface before commencing. A piece of 180 grade paper or similar will not spoil a smooth wood surface, but will give an opportunity to properly study and make a mental note of grain markings etc.

Fold the sandpaper once or twice to make it easier to grip, or, alternatively, wrap it around a smaller scrap of plywood. Work the sandpaper up and down the surface in the direction of the wood grain using just the weight of your hand. (Sanding against the grain will roughen the surface.) Try to run the sandpaper along the full length of the wood with each stroke.

Ensure that the surface you are sanding is away from the worktop you are using. This is because the sawdust from seasoned and kiln-dried timbers is dry, and fine-grade sandpaper produces a lot of wood dust over a period of time which can be an unpleasant irritant, making you sneeze.

Furthermore, sawdust on the surface of the wood you are about to pyrograph will occasionally build up as you are burning in the form of a carbon deposit. This will lower the temperature of the tip of the point until the little bit of carbon detaches itself, whereupon it will heat up again. This is normally only a problem when working on a small detail, slowly, and at a low temperature setting. Nevertheless,

before doing anything else, wipe the wood surface clean. The best thing to use for this purpose is a piece of corduroy cloth. I wear corduroy jeans a lot of the time when I am working, and persistently using the right trouser leg tends to wear them out. To avoid this problem I suggest cutting up a pair of jeans that have outlived their usefulness.

Finally, with a pair of scissors, cut out a 1in (13mm) square of the sandpaper and attach it to the top corner of the wood. This will save you having to look for a piece of sandpaper next time you wish to remove any traces of carbon from the point before attempting a detailed part of your work.

Before you begin any exercise, make sure you have a spare scrap of wood nearby of the same species as the one you are working on. Keep testing the point of your tool on this until you are sure it is going to produce the effect you want.

Getting into the habit of following these simple procedures will certainly save you time, and reduce the risk of spoiling a piece of work.

The right sort of light

To appreciate more easily the effect that creating a texture on the wood surface has, it is worth getting into the habit of working under a small angle-poise worklamp. If a light is directed across the surface that is being pyrographed, the minute shadows formed by the varying depths of the marks can show the overall textured effect as it is being formed. Finished pyrographs containing some of the more deeply engraved textures take on a three-dimensional quality when displayed with the correctly angled lighting. The best pyrography I have seen – and not all of them are contemporary works – are those pyrographs composed using a range of light and dark marks and lines, where a clear attempt has been

made to pyrograph textures and tones that correspond with actual subjects. This may be a little difficult to comprehend at this early stage, but after a little practice and experimentation it will become clearer.

■ Starting out with the hot-wire machine

Setting the temperature of the point

Once the technique of making a good strong point has been mastered, the next stage is to find an average temperature setting and then try the point out. The easiest way to do this is to hold the pencil in one hand and slowly turn the heat control dial up with the other hand. You will notice as you turn the dial that the point of the pencil soon becomes red hot (*see* Fig 5.1). The transformer concentrates the heat at the tip of the point which is why the pencil handle never gets hot and uncomfortable to hold. As soon as the tip is glowing red, slowly turn the dial down until it ceases to glow. You are now ready to begin.

A simple exercise

The wood surface is prepared, the wire point is set to an average temperature; you are now ready to produce your first pyrographed marks. For the purposes of this first and simple exercise there are just two rules that need apply:

1 Do not 'write' with the pencil. This is an enormous temptation. At craft demonstrations over the years many people have asked to try out the pyrography pencil, and their first reaction

Fig 5.1 A red-hot point.

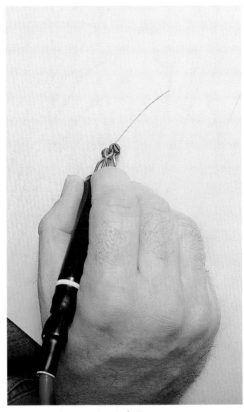

Fig 5.2 Producing a fine, light line.

is always to write. This, in a way, is a tribute to the equipment. The pyrography pencil is so light, it feels like a pen. So, to begin with at least, *no* writing.
2 Do not draw, sketch, or produce anything that can be identified. In other words all you need to do at the outset is doodle. I often ask students at this early stage of the proceedings to imagine that instead of a piece of plywood before them they have a new copy of the *Yellow Pages*, while at the same time they are listening to an extremely boring person on the phone.

Without altering the temperature setting on the transformer, make a series of lines and marks. There are many different ways you can do this. For example, if you apply the point to the wood gently, and move it swiftly along the surface, you will produce a fine, light line (*see* Fig 5.2). If, on the other hand, you use a little more pressure and move the wire across the wood slowly, you will obtain a much broader, darker line (*see*

Fig 5.1 A red-hot point.

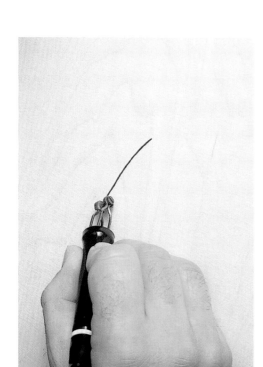

point. If you press too hard the point will probably bend (*see* Fig 5.5). If this happens, turn the point round and press it back into position on a scrap piece of wood. The nichrome wire is very pliable and it is unlikely that you will break it.

Drawing or engraving?

Pyrography is a compromise between drawing and engraving, but it is closer to the engraver's art than the illustrator's. The reproduction of texture is what the good pyrographer is after, rather than brown marks on top of wooden surfaces. To this end, modern pyrography tools can sometimes work against you. They are safe and simple to use, and it is too easy to produce at speed an illustration that could just as easily have been executed with a brown pen.

Any pyrography pencil or tool is able to produce a variety of light and dark marks on a wooden surface, but so much more is possible if you consider the

Fig 5.3 (left)
Producing a broad, dark line.
Fig 5.4 (below)
Blobbing.

Fig 5.3). It naturally follows that a whole range of different thicknesses can be achieved depending on the pressure and speed applied. Continue with this for a while, and see how many varied lines you can make.

Blobbing

Along with practically everyone who tries this exercise for the first time you will have noticed that even a short line is rarely produced without the occurrence of 'blobbing'. Your short line has a blob at the start and finish (*see* Fig 5.4). This is because you are working with a piece of metal that is continually burning the wood, as opposed to a Biro for example, which supplies an even flow of ink. With a little practice this problem can easily be overcome. Allow the point to arrive in contact with the wood as if it was an aircraft coming in to land. Then when you get to the end of the line, however short, let the point 'take off' again. Remember that as long as the wire is in contact with the wood it will be burning it.

Do not be afraid to press hard with the

engraving potential. For example, deeper pyrographed lines will create tiny shadows which collectively can suggest fur, feathers, bark, grass and a host of other tones and textures, none of which would be as easy to show using mediums such as watercolour, charcoal or pencil (*see* Fig 5.6).

So, right from the very beginning, keep the idea of engraving firmly in your mind and you will almost certainly avoid the kind of boring, transparent pyrography often seen at craft venues. If your pyrography has that 'brown pen' look about it, you have not been keeping the word 'engrave' in your thoughts.

This natural tendency of students to use the pyrography tool as a pen is possibly the only disadvantage of modern electrical tools. Pyrographers of the 19th century and earlier had more basic equipment, but this did at least enable them to produce a variety of very deep marks, often working on wall panels with only a flickering candle to see by. This way they would have seen very quickly the potential effects obtained by engraving, rather than simply producing uniform burned lines.

Creating textures

Be as imaginative as you can with your doodling. Try to group tiny areas of marks together to form different areas of

Fig 5.5 (below)
A bent point.
Fig 5.6 (right)
All sorts of effects, including this feather texture, are possible with the pyrography tool, when it is used as an engraving device.

texture. Try holding the pencil at different angles so that the point also meets the wood at different angles. You will quickly realize that the point is far less likely to bend under pressure when applied to the wood at an angle. Indeed it is possible to cut quite deep lines into the wood surface by using the point slightly on its side.

See how black you can make a small area of texture. One way of doing this is to

create dots that gradually build into a cluster. Make sure that each dot joins the next dot, and a solid dark area will result. You can then repeat this process, only working more quickly, if you want to produce a lighter version of the same texture.

If you have followed all the hints and suggestions for this doodle so far, you should now be able to step back and see a good range of light and dark blobs, marks and hopefully small areas of texture. If you are satisfied with these early efforts, repeat some of them with the temperature of the point increased. There is no need to turn the temperature right up until the point is glowing brightly. As the point gets hotter, it will become more pliable and more likely to bend. It is also difficult to work accurately with a red-hot point. This is because the hotter the point is, the faster it will burn.

However, you will find there are some interesting effects obtainable with 'overburning': at an increased temperature setting you will often find

Fig 5.7
Overburning.

the marks you are making have a halo of light-brown scorch marks around them (*see* Fig 5.7). This is overburning. In most cases it is not desirable, but like many of the accidents that occurred when I started my own pyrography, it is just another effect that in the right circumstances, can be put to good use.

■ Starting out with the solid-point machine

Much of the preceding information in this chapter is applicable to the solid-point machine also. In fact the only points that don't apply are those concerning

temperature setting, and the problem of 'blobbing', both of which are peculiar to hot-wire machine.

Regarding temperature setting, I recommend that you always set your solid-point machine at its maximum temperature. This is because the transformer has a larger area of metal to heat which then cools more rapidly on contact with a wood surface. Blobbing, for this same reason, is not a problem with solid-point machines.

For the purposes of carrying out the aforementioned exercise (*see* page 27) using the Janik G4 solid-point machine, the point I recomend is the B21. This point has a surface area at the tip that is nearest in size to a hot-wire machine point. When you have exhausted the doodling possibilities of this exercise, turn to pages 49 and 50 in Chapter 6. You may like to follow the instructions for Squares 5C, 5D, 6C and 6D, which are all created with the B21 point, as part of this first simple exercise.

■ Changing the points

To change a point on the hot-wire machine, *first switch off* the machine and allow it to cool for a while. Then loosen the terminal screws taking care not to bend the terminal support struts. Remove the old point and replace it with a new point or, alternatively, a short loop of wire. Tighten the terminal screws again making sure that you do not bend the terminal support struts. If necessary, squeeze the point into shape with pliers.

If you are intending to do a lot of work with different points, it may be worth buying a spare pencil to hold another point, and plugging it into the power unit when needed rather than having to continually change points on the pencil.

Changing the point of a solid-point tool requires less dexterity than in the case of hot-wire machines, and is mostly a matter of common sense. First, switch the machine off at the mains, but be warned – the point will remain very hot indeed for a considerable amount of time. If you prefer not to wait for it to cool down, the easiest and quickest way is to use a wooden clothes peg to grip and unscrew the point.

CHAPTER 6

The Sampler

In *A Guide To Poker Work* by W. D. Thompson, published at the turn of the century, there appears a specimen panel or sampler, containing a number of different backgrounds suitable for various kinds of illustrative work. It is one of the best examples I have seen of the kind of relief work that distinguishes pyrography from other visual artforms.

■ A learning tool

The sampler always seemed to me a natural way of allowing pyrography students to discover the potential of this medium for themselves. I have produced several samplers over the years before I ever spotted the panel in Thompson's book. It is the next stage in the teaching of beginners, and is always included in one form or another on my courses.

Samplers are interesting things to do, and it is important that you attempt one early on. There are two of them in this chapter, and simple directions have been provided for those who wish to duplicate some of the squares I have created. However, the best way of learning is to experiment. Even following the simple rules I suggest, you will find that the variety of tone and texture you can create in each square is practically endless. A completed sampler is always worth keeping as it can be used for reference in future work.

■ Marking out the blank

On a piece of sanded birch-faced plywood, mark out a grid of 24 1in (13mm) squares – six across and four down. Use a not-too-sharp, soft pencil – a B or 2B is suitable. Press very gently with the pencil so that the squares are only just visible as guidelines. If the pencil is too sharp it is likely to make an impression in the wood that will be difficult to erase. Likewise, a pencil line or mark that is too heavy can also be resistant to erasure, especially if a line has been pyrographed near to it; when this happens a reaction takes place with the heat of the point to render the pencil mark permanent.

■ A general guide to producing a sampler

1 Each of the 1in (13mm) squares must be filled completely with a different area of tone or texture.
2 Keep each square as simple and uncomplicated as possible. In other words make each square a consistent area.
3 Take your time; try to finish each square without any unpyrographed wood showing.
4 Try to produce an area of tone or texture on at least one square that goes from dark through to light or vice versa.

5 Avoid 'clever' patterns; in fact avoid all patterns other than those that you can claim as textures.

6 Produce at least one square that is as black as you can make it.

7 Use all of the variables at your disposal in terms of speed and heat control.

8 When you have finished a square, always write down a description of how you achieved the particular tone or texture in that square, including details of temperature, pressure and technique. In this way, the sampler becomes a useful reference source for the future.

■ A sampler using the hot-wire pyrography machine

The sampler for the hot-wire machine was divided into two sections. The 12 squares on the right-hand side were all produced with a spoon point; the 12 to the left, with a conventional wire point (*see* Fig 6.1).

Fig 6.1
A sampler using the hot-wire pyrography machine.

wire point spoon point

Fig 6.2
Plan of a hot-wire sampler.

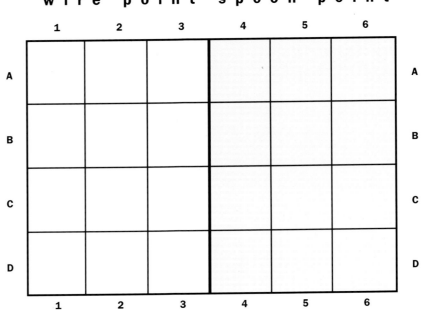

Conventional point

1A

Use a temperature setting that allows you to work slowly with some pressure, but not hot enough to burn a very dark line. Start by producing a series of close lines, working against the grain until you have filled the square. Repeat the same process, this time with the grain. You will need to reduce the temperature very slightly when working with the grain; this is because the point is not so obstructed and will burn more readily.

2A

The temperature needs to be fairly high for this square. Set the point so that it glows pink, then reduce the temperature slightly until the pink glow disappears. Working with the direction of the grain, apply the point positively to the surface for a second and then pull it away from the edge of the square towards the middle, gradually increasing the speed and at the same time reducing the pressure. Repeat this all the way down one side of the square. Make sure with each stroke of the point that you cease to have contact with the surface around the half way mark. You will find it easier to produce these flick strokes if you position the surface in such a way that you are pulling the point towards you. Carry on in the same way down the opposite side of the square.

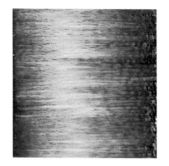

3A

Set the point until it is glowing slightly. Starting on any edge of the square, push the hot point into the surface holding the pencil more or less vertically. Work your way around all four edges of the square pushing the point into the surface in as identical a way as possible. When you have completed one circuit, start another one on the inside of the first, and so on until the square is completed. You will find it easier to produce even lines if you turn the board at the end of each completed row.

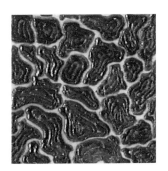

1B

Using a slightly lower temperature setting, similar to the one used in 1A, mark out with the point a series of varying shapes that are interspaced equally. If you are nervous of doing this with the point, use a soft pencil. Working slowly, and with an increase in the pressure, work the point around each outline to produce a nice, positive, dark line. Then move inwards, burning another line adjacent to the previous one until you have worked your way to the middle of the shape and thus completely filled it. Repeat the process with the other shapes until each one becomes its own little island of dark texture.

2B

Working *with* the grain, this particular type of mark is made with the point making contact with the surface at an angle of approximately 45 degrees and then being pulled carefully towards you. The purpose of this is to use as much of the broad part of the point as possible to make a wider mark. Using a soft pencil and ruler, mark in the direction of the grain a series of lines roughly a millimetre apart – these are just a guide. Set the temperature high enough to give you a positive dark line while working quite slowly and pressing fairly hard. Start at the top of the square, pulling the point towards you, but breaking the line at random intervals. Work your way down the square in this way creating a 'brickwork' effect. Turn the temperature down significantly, and repeat the process, this time working on the areas previously left. The density of colour will be determined by the pressure and temperature settings used.

3B

The effect in this square can best be achieved by using the side of the tip of the point. With a soft pencil, carefully draw 10 to 12 wavy lines at random from the top to the bottom of the square. Set the temperature of the point fairly low and practise on a scrap of ply until you can produce a fine but positive line. Start from either side of the square with a row of lines leading from the edge to the first wavy line. Continue along the square with the next set of lines angled in the opposite direction, and then produce a further set of lines at a similar angle to the first. The square you see in my sampler was started from the right-hand side, and all of the first lines seemed more or less equidistant. As you progress across you will see that, because of the wavy lines, the gaps widen in some areas, which adds interest to this area of texture.

1C

Increase the temperature of the point until it is clearly glowing pink. Start in the middle of the square making short marks in random directions that touch each other. You will have to work fairly quickly because at this heat the point will burn into the wood very rapidly. Try to ensure that each mark is made in the same way with the point in contact with the surface for the same length of time. This kind of square needs to be completed in one go. A lot of smoke will be flying off the wood; if this is a problem and makes your eyes water, you can disperse it by gently blowing towards the offending area. Try not to blow too hard, cooling the point, as this will obviously affect the consistency of the burning. Because of the intensity of the burning it is very difficult to confine it as you work close to the edges of the square. Work the square as close as you can to the edge, and then turn the heat down slightly. By this means you will be able to slow down and work more accurately along the edge to complete the square.

2C

Again use the point at the setting that makes it glow pink. A little practice on your scrap piece is a good idea; the hot tip of the point needs to be applied with a modicum of pressure for the shortest possible time. As soon as the point has made contact it needs to be pulled away from the surface; in other words, a flick stroke. The easiest way to describe this without the luxury of a live demonstration is to compare it with a comma when writing with a Biro. Once you are satisfied that you can produce this mark, the object is to repeat as many identical ones as you can, keeping them fairly evenly spaced to complete the square.

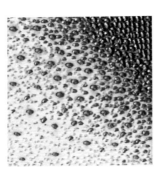

3C

This square has been created by using dots formed with the point set at a reasonably high temperature setting. All the dots have been made at the same temperature, but at differing speeds. The point needs to be set until it glows very slightly, and then turned down until there is no visible glow. Start at the top right-hand corner producing dots slowly and with a little pressure. As you move towards the opposite side of the square, spread them further apart. Repeat the process, reducing the time the point is in contact with the surface and therefore reducing the density of the dot. Repeat once more, this time just touching the surface.

1D

Lightly draw with a soft pencil a series of equally spaced lines going down the square. Using the same temperature as you did in 3C, mark a series of lines slowly in a row going from left to right between the top of the square and the first pencil line. Use enough pressure and speed to make positive dark lines. Repeat again with the row beneath, but speed up enough to produce significantly lighter marks. Repeat again with the third row even more lightly. Produce another three lines graded in the same way as the first three, and so on until the square is completed.

2D

Turn the surface in a way that allows you to pull the point towards you with the grain. Set the temperature low enough to make it difficult to produce a heavily burnt line. It is important that you are able to exert the maximum pressure with the point without bending it. Use the flat of the point and draw it towards you. Try and push as deep a groove as possible into the surface. Repeat each line as near to the previous one as possible without necessarily forming straight lines.

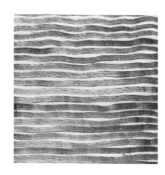

3D

This is quite a difficult area of tone to produce, but it is worth attempting because there are many applications for this particular skill. Leave the temperature setting low, using just enough heat to scorch the wood if you were using the point to write. Position the end of the point on its side slightly, or at an angle. This will mean that less of the point will make contact with the surface, and a thinner line will result than in square 2D. Push the point with as much pressure as you can, and in as many directions as possible, all over the square. Try and direct your efforts towards severely marking the surface rather than burning it. The difficulty with this is maintaining a consistency over the whole square. You need to work quickly and continuously so that the heat of the point is absorbed by the surface. If you stop for a rest, even for a couple of seconds, the point will reheat and, when reapplied, will burn the surface more severely than before. This problem can be overcome by blowing gently on the point as you are about to make contact. Once you have completed your square with a consistent area of tone, start working from the top again, but far more slowly. The point will fall into the grooves already made and you will easily be able to produce a dark-to-light effect down the square.

Spoon point

4A
Turn the surface so that you can pull the spoon point towards you with the grain. Set the temperature to an average heat, i.e. the spoon is not glowing. Using the edge of the spoon point like a knife, pull it towards you, cutting a line from one side of the square to the other. You will find this quite easy with the grain – the wood offers very little resistance. Repeat the lines one after the other as near to each other as possible until the square is filled.

5A
Increase the temperature until there is a slight glow from the spoon point. Holding the pencil in a more vertical position, push the tip of the point into the surface. Repeat this in a similar way all over the square leaving a visible gap between each mark. Using a lot of heat like this produces an overburning effect around the mark you are making so that, although you are spacing the marks, the surface between each mark is singed.

6A
Squares 5A and 6A should really be attempted together. They are produced in a similar way, though the results are very different, demonstrating the range of marks, tones and textures possible in a sampler. You will need more care and control with this square. Turn the temperature down slightly from the setting you used on 5A. Produce a similar but more careful mark with the tip of the spoon point, then repeat this, producing a row of identical marks next to each other along the top of the square. Angle the marks to the right for the first line, to the left for the second line, to the right again for the third line, and so on. Take all the time you need and ensure that all the marks are done in as similar a way as possible. Work your way down until the square is completed.

4B

This is an easy square to do providing you show care and patience. The most important thing here is to set the temperature absolutely right. It does not need to be that hot – just enough to produce a very black mark with the convex side of the spoon point pushed positively down on the surface. It might be worth experimenting on a scrap of the surface to get it right before you start the square. Start in the middle and carefully produce each mark so it just touches the previous mark. Try not to go over the top of the mark as you may actually remove some of the burning. You will almost certainly experience a build-up of carbon on the spoon point; this can be removed by *gently* stroking the point's surface on an old piece of sandpaper. I say gently because too much abrasion will rough up the surface of the point and make it more susceptible to the collecting of unwanted carbon deposits. Turn the temperature down slightly when you come to work around the edge of the square, but remember to increase the time and pressure with each of these final marks to compensate. The end result should be a very black square with a texture like beaten pewter.

5B

The convex side of the spoon point is used again for this square, though set at a much lower temperature. The idea is to singe the surface of the wood in a fairly even way without applying too much pressure. Starting somewhere in the middle, gently shade the surface in a circular motion, moving on when the required depth of colour has been achieved. This is by no means as easy as it appears; to linger too long on one spot will mean uneven burning. As with several other squares, it will pay you to try to finish it in one go. To remove the point from the surface for a second and reapply it will give it time to heat up to a fiercer temperature. A low heat setting gives you the control necessary to work carefuly and slowly. Continue until the square is completed.

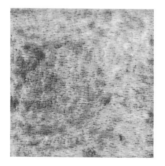

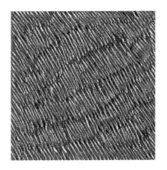

6B

Looking at a completed example of this square would tell you little about how it was created. The first stage is exactly the same as the process for 5B only with a higher temperature setting. This will result in a darker version of 5B. Then, using the edge of the spoon point, cut through the singed surface from one corner in a shading motion. You will find this easier if you cover a short area of approximately ⅜in (10mm) at a time. The hot edge of the point is effectively removing the singed surface, or etching into it. You may have to stop occasionally to remove the collected particles of surface and carbon that build up on the edge of the point. Continue with this until the square is completed.

4C

Turn up the temperature until the point is glowing red hot. Remember that any higher than this renders the point useless and, apart from making the metal very soft, it could melt. At this temperature you only have to touch the surface to get a very positive mark surrounded by the yellowish colour of singed wood. After the obligatory practice on a scrap piece of material, make a series of short lines over the square with plenty of space around each mark. Turn the surface slightly and repeat the process so that the next set of marks is in a different direction. By the time you have done this two or three times you will not be able to make further marks without touching previous ones. Continue with the marks running into each other until the square is evenly balanced. The result should be a texture similar to a hedgehog's prickly coat.

5C

This square is probably easier to produce than to describe. The point needs to be set at a heat that will enable you to make a fairly dark mark by working slowly with a lot of pressure. Each individual mark should be dark at the beginning, tailing off as the heat of the point is absorbed by the surface and the pressure is reduced.

Once you have mastered this process, simply produce the marks in groups of three or four starting each set of subsequent lines at 90 degrees from the previous set. Continue until the square is completed.

6C

This area of shading or texture is achieved by reproducing the second stage of the square at 6B. Set at a moderate temperature (i.e. so that the point is hot but some way off actually glowing) and use a shading motion with the edge of the spoon point. You can either work on a small area at a time or, as I have done, work from the top left-hand corner down to the bottom right-hand corner.

4D

This is one of those squares that looks extremely complex and difficult to do, but is in fact very simple. All that is required is a combination of patience and confidence. Set the temperature of the point reasonably low and then, using the edge of the point, cut a short, dark line. As the edge cuts into the surface it will really do the work for you. You need to produce a series of groups of lines, identically spaced and at different angles. Make sure each group is isolated initially, and make sure you turn the surface to change the direction of the marks and not the pyrography pencil. The texture can be made to vary considerably depending on the weight of each of the tiny lines and the distance between them. Once you have produced ten or twelve series of marks, repeat the process again, linking up the groups. Continue with this until all the gaps have been filled.

5D

Using low temperature settings combined with pressure and slow deliberate movements, accuracy in pyrographic work is virtually guaranteed. This square requires all of these criteria if it is to be executed properly. Work diagonally, making sure you are travelling across the grain. Pyrographing along the grain is

always easier, but it is not always possible to do this. However, if you take your time at this low heat you will have no problem. Use the convex side of the spoon point, and pull it towards you across the surface. Carefully introduce a slight variation in the direction of the line as you go. Whether you begin in the middle of the square or in one corner, make sure that each line follows the previous line with just a small gap separating them. Take every care that the gap is, as far as possible, of equal width. As you move through the square try to vary the weight and pressure of the odd line for an added effect.

6D

The final square of this sampler is a variation on the square at 4B. Set the temperature in the same way as in 4B, and simply work a little faster using less pressure to produce a slightly elongated mark. The square at 6D quite often resembles an attempt at 4B where not enough patience was evident.

A sampler using the solid-point pyrography machine

This 24-square sampler has been produced to show the extensive range of tones and textures that are possible with a small selection of points (*see* Fig 6.3). The purpose of any sampler is to learn the scope and capabilities of the tools you are planning to use, and to record what has been discovered. If it is your intention from the outset to produce the type of pyrography that is more suited to this type of tool, then it is strongly recommended that you have a go at making a sampler like the one described below. This will give you an invaluable point of reference for the kinds of tone or texture that are available when you are faced with a specific pattern or area to be pyrographed. You could use several different points or, with a little

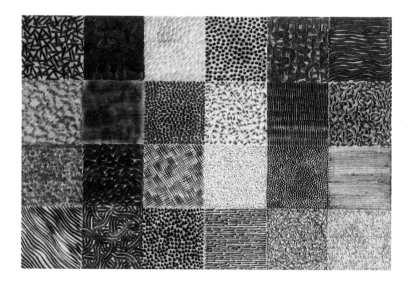

Fig 6.3
A sampler using the solid-point pyrography machine.

	1	2	3	4	5	6	
A	B22	P20	P20	22	B22	B24
B	B24	P20	B24	22	B22	B24
C	B24	P20	B22	22	B21	B21
D	B22	B24	B22	22	B21	B21

Fig 6.4
Plan of a solid-point sampler. The numbers in the squares refer to the points used to create the sampler shown in Fig 6.3.

imagination and by varying the heat and pressure, produce a sampler with just one point. It is not suggested that you copy exactly the squares produced here, but a brief explanation of how each square was produced may be helpful. Refer to Fig 6.4 to find out which point should be used in each square.

N.B. The temperature was at full heat for all of the squares.

1A

Using the sharp cutting edge of the point, push it firmly into the surface. Try to make sure each mark is made using the same amount of pressure and time in contact with the surface. Move the work surface round after several marks, and then again after several more marks, in order to create marks in many different directions.

1B

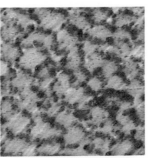

Working fairly rapidly, shade small areas of approximately ¼in (6mm) at a time. Rather than shade the whole square at one go, produce small shaded areas at random over the square, then fill in the gaps with more small shaded areas.

1C

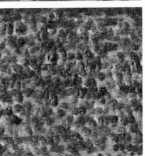

Working fairly rapidly and using the rounded end of the point, fill in the whole square without stopping if possible. Use a shading motion moving the point in as many different directions as you can. Continuous contact with the surface, will cool it. If you stop before the square is completed, blow on the end of the point just before you restart to avoid a fierce initial burn.

1D

Using the sharp cutting edge of the point cut a line from one corner of the square to the other. Twist it slightly and it will form a curve. Repeat this from the middle to one corner, and then the same to the other corner.

2A

Using the flat of the point, hold it on the surface for a short time until a very positive black mark is formed. Start towards the middle of the square and work outwards. The point you are using has a straight side that you can use at the edges of the square. With this intense type of burning, deposits of wood carbon will form on the flat of the point. These can be removed by gently rubbing against a piece of sandpaper.

2B

Gently and speedily rub the flat of the point over the surface. Use the minimum of pressure to create an untextured shading effect.

2C

Using the front end of the flat of the point, push it into the surface to give a deep burn from the tip of the point that fades in intensity as the point separates from the surface. Keep repeating the same mark until the square is covered.

2D

Push the point fairly firmly into the surface to produce lines in groups of three. Make approximately six similar detached groups of these lines, then turn the surface round and repeat the exercise making your second set of lines appear to weave from the first set. Turn the board again and repeat until the square is completed.

3A
Using the tip of the point at an angle that prevents the flat coming into contact with the surface, make brief contact, pulling the point towards you. Continue with this whilst trying to ensure that all the marks are as similar as possible. The best way to do this is to complete the square without stopping.

3B
Push the rounded end of the point vertically into the surface. Repeat to fill the square, trying to ensure that the same pressure is used for each mark, and that all the marks are roughly the same distance apart, to produce a uniform area of texture.

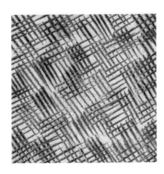

3C
Using the cutting edge of the point and working quickly with moderate pressure, produce groups of five or six short lines. Repeat this at equidistant intervals over the square until the total area of lines equals the area of untouched surface. The easiest way to do this is to pull the point towards you. Turn the surface through 90 degrees and then repeat the exercise, filling all the gaps until the square is filled.

3D
Push the end of the cutting edge gently into the surface to produce this triangular-shaped mark. Repeat the mark until the square is covered.

4A

Push the point vertically into the surface. The amount of pressure used will determine the depth and therefore the size of the mark. Repeat at intervals until the square is covered. The density of this area of tone can be altered by changing the size of the spaces between the marks.

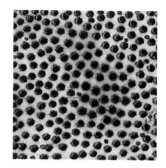

4B

Apply the point at an angle to the surface. Make the briefest of contacts before flicking the point away. Repeat this in as many different directions as possible to produce a square of uniform texture.

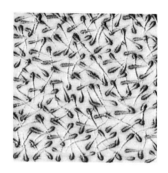

4C

Apply the tip of the point with very little pressure while keeping it moving all the time. Scribble over the surface, changing direction constantly. Try and complete the square in one go. If you have to stop for any reason, gently blow on the point immediately before reapplying it to the surface.

4D

In the direction of the grain, push the tip of the point into the surface and pull it towards you for a short distance before breaking and continuing. Repeat this working your way down the square making sure the breaks occur at different points with each line.

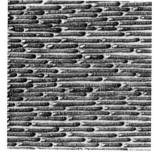

5A

Instead of using the cutting edge of this point to cut with, drag the edge across the surface to make each mark. Work your way from left to right, leaving between each mark a space equal to the size of the mark. When you reach the bottom of the square, turn the surface through 90 degrees and repeat the whole exercise again, working through the original marks.

5B

Using approximately half of the point's cutting edge, i.e. placing the point at an angle to the surface, make a row of short cuts across the top of the square. Produce a similar row immediately below the first and so on until the square is completed.

5C

Push the tip of the point vertically into the surface and keep repeating the same mark. Try to ensure that all the marks are very close to each other, if not actually touching.

5D

Apply the point at an angle to the surface and drag it a short distance before removing it from the surface. Repeat the same movement until the square is filled, varying the direction as often as possible. This same effect can be created by keeping the point in contact with the surface until the square is completed, but if you opt for this you must try and complete the square in one go. Unlike the method described for 4C, you need to apply pressure, and this makes it difficult to continue for a whole area without a break.

6A

Start in the middle of the side of the square and position the surface so you are able to pull the point towards you with the grain. Give the lines a deliberate wave, leaving the odd small gap as you progress across the square. As with some previous squares, the density will be determined by the size of the gaps between each line.

6B

Apply the point at an angle to the surface. Make positive but brief contact before flicking the point away. Repeat this in as many directions as possible to produce a uniform square.

6C

Use as much pressure as is comfortable and work quickly to build up a series of identical, touching lines. Work in the direction of the grain and position the surface so that you can pull the point towards you.

6D

Even at a high temperature setting it is difficult with this particular point to burn a very dark line. Use plenty of pressure and speed in a scribbling motion. Try to produce a texture on the surface with the pressure you are applying rather than relying on the heat of the point to burn. This will give you an area of texture which is uniform but not particularly dark.

CHAPTER 7

A Simple Composition

The following exercise is designed to show how what has been discovered so far can be applied to a simple piece of work, while at the same time getting to grips with the problem that torments many beginners: how to produce a constant and continuous line.

▨ Bunch of grasses

Fig 7.1
A collection of grasses taped to a piece of ply.

To begin with, go out and pick a varied bunch of grasses, weeds and anything else growing in the garden or by the

roadside with an interesting appearance. Arrange your collection in a receptacle where it can easily be viewed – or better still, attach a row of your cuttings with masking tape to a large piece of card or ply (*see* Fig 7.1).

Prepare a piece of birch-faced plywood with an approximate size of 5 x 7in (127 x 178mm) (*see* page 25). If you have several pieces of wood to choose from, here is your first opportunity to pick the surface best suited for the proposed composition. In this case, the ideal surface will have the grain running lengthwise rather than from side to side.

Engraving the stems

With the wood placed so that the grain runs vertically, engrave near the bottom a series of lines to represent the stems of your grasses. Make sure that some of the lines reach a point approximately two thirds of the way up the wood. Engrave at least five or six lines to begin with. You can use a little artistic licence and allow the lines to 'wave in the wind' slightly (*see* Fig 7.2).

It will soon become clear that this apparently simple task is in fact quite difficult. The following are some alternative ways of engraving straight lines. Simply choose the method you find easiest:

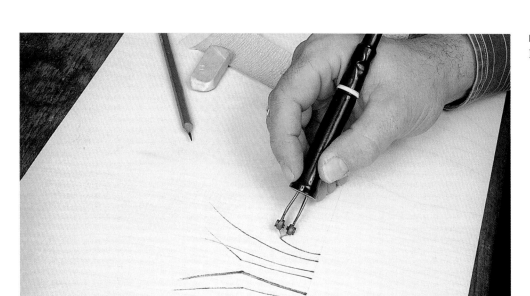

Fig 7.2
Engraving the lines.

- Use the side of the wire, an average-to-low temperature setting and a fair amount of pressure.
- Either push the wire along the wood or, if you find it easier, turn the wood around and pull the point slowly towards you.
- Make a groove in the surface by engraving quickly with pressure, to create a line that is only lightly burnt. You can then use this groove, following its course more slowly and deliberately, to produce the desired effect: a straight line.
- A reasonably long line can be produced in sections, each an inch or so in length. Providing each section overlaps with the preceding section, the line will appear unbroken.

Producing reasonable lines in pyrography requires lots of practice, so do not worry if you cannot get a good result straight away. Remember to take your time, do not use too much heat, and maintain an even pressure. The wire or point will burn into the surface at a rate precisely in accordance with the duration of its contact with the wood. In other words, if you falter or jerk as your pull the point along the surface, you can expect an uneven and inconsistent line. It is always easier to work with the grain of the wood; the grain tends to obstruct a point that is travelling across it. It is possible to pyrograph a line through the grain, but this requires even less heat, more pressure and a slow and deliberate fight against it. One of the reasons for recommending birch-faced plywood to beginners is that the surface offers less resistance to the point.

Engraving the seed sections

Now you should have before you a piece of wood hopefully engraved with some stems. Choose one of the pieces of grass and study it carefully, taking particular notice of how the seed or fruit section at the top is composed. The idea is not to draw or copy what is before you, but to find a way of suggesting the subject by means of pyrography. You already have a whole range of marks and textures at your disposal, gleaned from the previous exercises (*see* Chapters 5 and 6). See if you can use these discoveries – or combinations of various marks – to create a graphic representation of your chosen subject.

The textures described for Square 2C on page 37, and Square 4B on page 48

Fig 7.3 (right)
Executing a flick stroke.
Fig 7.4 (far right)
The finished pyrograph.

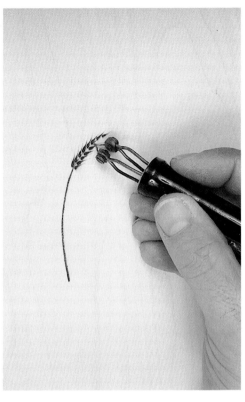

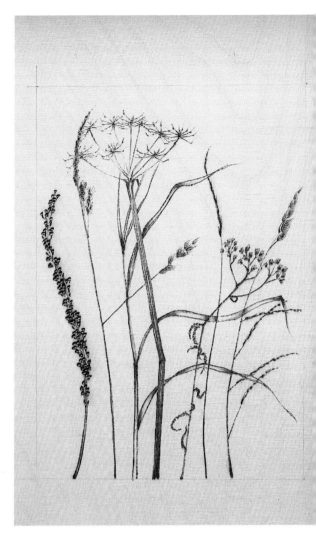

provide the key to this. Many wild grass seeds, wild barley, wheat and similarly formed flora, have seeds which can be represented pyrographically by pushing the point into the wood and drawing it swiftly out and along to form something that can be described as a blob with a hair growing out of one end (*see* Fig 7.3). This 'flick stroke' crops up in various guises and is a useful thing to be able to do. It is therefore worth spending some time practising it.

The more interesting pyrographs are always the ones that show a range of light and dark tones, textures and lines. Do not fall into the trap at this stage of making all your work a compilation of similarly weighted lines and marks. Look at the different grasses etc. and try to ensure that you create dark areas and marks where they occur, interspersed with lighter and more delicate work (*see* Fig 7.4).

If you are not satisfied with the samples of grasses etc. that you have collected, it would not be unreasonable to design some of your own. At this stage

you need not worry about reproducing exact likenesses of the subject; it is more a case of suggesting the subject. This exercise is intended to be a progression from the previous exercises, using and applying what has already been learnt, and gaining practice in producing consistent and positive pyrographed lines. So feel free to invent away.

Adding depth

Having successfully arrived at this stage, let us consider how this composition can be improved by adding a little depth to it. Now that you are well into your first pyrograph, you may have some interesting ideas of your own. Here are three suggestions based on ideas I use myself:

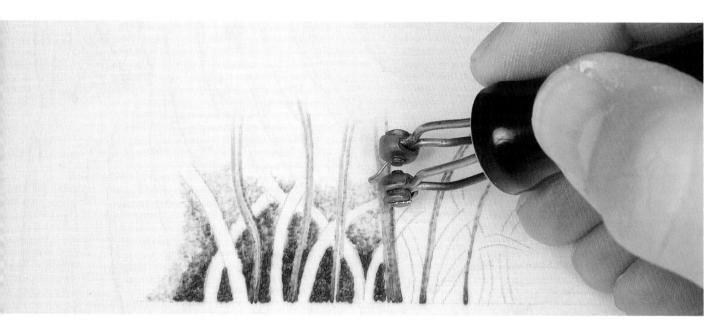

1 Working from the bottom of the pyrograph, carefully draw with a B pencil a series of vertical lines to represent blades of grass or similar. Make it interesting, allowing the lines to weave and overlap occasionally. Make sure you apply the pencil very gently so that you will be able to erase where necessary. Recalling Squares 3C and 3D from the hot-wire sampler (see pages 37 and 38) that dealt with tones changing from dark to light, pyrograph behind each blade of grass, again starting at the bottom, beginning with a very black tone and gradually fading into a lighter tone (see Fig 7.5). There are various ways of tackling this:

■ Using a dot texture, either gradually increase your speed as you work your way up the design, or else decrease the temperature of the point at intervals, thus creating a light-to-dark effect.

■ Use virtually any simple texture, or even a simple pattern, as long as the effect is one of gradual tonal change. This pyrographed background will give your composition some depth, especially if you make the dark areas as black as possible at the bottom of the design, as shown in the samplers (see Chapter 6). You will appreciate from this how the most interesting pyrographs are usually the ones that

boast a wide range of light and dark tones and effects.

2 Repeat the process described above, but substitute the B pencil lines for pyrographed lines. When you have an arrangement of blades of grass weaving and overlapping, instead of working on the areas of wood behind the subject, shade in the parts of the subject you would normally expect to be in shadow. This shading effect is another way of adding depth to the design. It can most easily be achieved with the spoon point, but feel free to use whichever method you prefer.

Many types of grass, especially when dried, have interesting leaf formations, rather as if the blades of grass have been twisted into ribbons. These can also be added to the composition by using this second method, but showing the leaves starting from the actual stem. They will appear all the more interesting if you can use a little imagination, and weave them in and around other stems and grasses (see Fig 7.6).

3 The third suggestion is probably the easiest; it is certainly the quickest and least complicated. It involves the use of the spoon point. With the temperature at an average-to-low setting and using the

Fig 7.5
Suggestion 1. You can add depth by drawing in blades of grass at the base of your illustration and pyrographing dark-fading-gradually-to-light tones behind these.

largest surface area of the spoon point, burn a series of slow, deliberate and – as far as possible – black lines from the bottom of the design. Again, make them interesting and realistic by allowing them to wave around a little. Weave them in and out of each other as you might expect to find them growing. When you have completed this, burn some fairly lengthy and gradually fading strokes from the base of the design and through the dark original lines (*see* Fig 7.7).

These are three suggestions for effects that I have often used. These ideas can be combined, or you can easily invent your own.

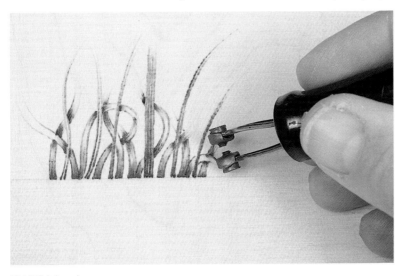

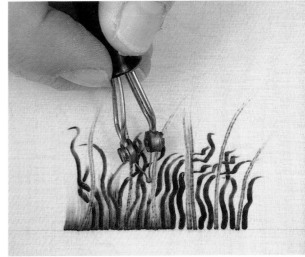

Fig 7.6 (above)
Suggestion 2. Pyrograph blades of grass at the base, then shade in the shadow areas using the spoon point.
Fig 7.7 (right)
Suggestion 3. Also at the base, interweave some black wavy lines and a few longer, gradually fading strokes.

CHAPTER 8

Tracing and Pyrographing a Butterfly

Tracing is too often referred to as cheating. Far from cheating, it is a most effective way of accurately planning an illustration, and not just for pyrographic work; I believe that in any art or craft, it is the result that is important, and not necessarily how it was arrived at. (Please read the note on page v before copying material for your own use.)

■ How to make a tracing for pyrography

There are various ways of tracing. Most well known is the heavy soft pencil on the back of the master, and then redrawing the piece of work. The method I use was learned from a glass engraver I worked with some years ago. I was intrigued by this man's work, and in particular the accuracy of his copies of old engravings onto glass goblets, bearing in mind that he only used a simple hand engraving tool and not the more commonly used electric equipment.

The area of the glass to be engraved was painted with white emulsion. This would dry quickly, as the paint had nothing to key into. A photocopy was made of the original piece of work, reduced or enlarged to fit the area to be engraved. This was then attached to the glass and held in position from the top by ordinary masking tape. A small piece of old, well-used black pencil carbon paper was then inserted face down between the emulsion and the photocopy. Using a sharp, hard pencil, the relevant parts were then traced directly onto the emulsion. If the area to be engraved was curved, as you might expect on a glass, goblet or bowl, an allowance could be made for this by making some small cuts in the photocopy and bending it around the object's surface. (Naturally this same principle can be applied to rounded wooden objects.) Having traced the essential details of the original, taking care to reproduce the main lines and marks that gave proportions and dimensions, the carbon paper and photocopy were removed and the marks made in carbon scratched into the glass. It was then a simple matter of washing off the emulsion and engraving in the illustration.

I soon realized the application of this tracing technique to pyrography was going to save me a lot of time, especially when several similar items had to be pyrographed with the same illustration. To transfer by this method onto wood is obviously a lot easier than onto glass. Naturally there is no need for the

Fig 8.1
Butterfly template.

emulsion, although extra care has to be taken to ensure that no marks are traced that are not going to be burnt away.

So why not give this time-saver a try. You will need:

- A small piece of black pencil carbon paper, preferably one that has been well used.
- A hard pencil, as sharp as you can make it. A 2H pencil is best, sharpened with a pencil sharpener, followed by a Stanley knife or scalpel.
- A simple photocopy of a line drawing. It does not matter what drawing or original you use for this exercise, as long as it is a line illustration, preferably simple to follow and not a photograph. Fig 8.1 is a good example. Photocopy paper is the ideal thickness for tracing in this way and, if you are careful, you will be able to use the same one several times.
- Masking tape. Never use Sellotape – it will almost certainly lift tiny pieces of the wood surface when you are removing it. Masking tape has a less sticky surface and will not leave a gum deposit on the wood.

■ Butterfly

Tracing the butterfly

If you have decided to use a photocopy of the butterfly illustration in Fig 8.1, cut the image out leaving a little bit of white paper around it. This will give you an edge to attach it to the wood surface. You should have enough space in the upper areas of the previous exercise (*see* Chapter 7) to fit the butterfly in as part of that composition. However, if you prefer, prepare another piece of birch-faced plywood (*see* page 25).

Decide the best position for the butterfly and attach the master to the wood surface. Place the piece of pencil carbon paper underneath the master. Be very careful once the carbon paper is in position not to press too hard with any part of your hand, and be extra careful if you are wearing a ring or bracelet. It is very easy to make carbon marks where you do not want them, but not so easy to remove them.

With the sharpened 2H pencil, carefully follow the outline of the butterfly's top wing – just one short, precise line (*see* Fig 8.2). Lift up the master without altering its position, and check the line you have just traced. The line you should see is fine and faint – in fact you should hardly be able to see it. If the line is too dark, you have pressed too hard. If the line is too broad, you may have pressed too hard, but it is more likely that the pencil is not sharp enough. Pressing too hard will also dent the wood slightly, which is also something to avoid.

Continue until the whole butterfly has been traced, checking periodically that you are still getting a fine faint line. If the carbon paper has been fairly well worked on then it is likely that the carbon will not have been used up evenly. Mark in the two dots to represent the antennae, but do not put the actual antennae in yet. A good way of checking that none of the detail has been missed is to lift the master up and down rapidly, comparing it with the

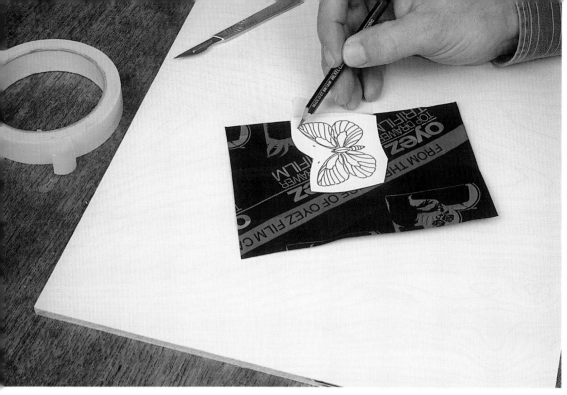

tracing (rather like a 'flick' picture). If you
are satisfied that nothing has been missed
out, you can peel off the master.

Antennae

It is now time to pyrograph. You can only
expect to get one attempt at pyrographing
the antennae, which is why it is best to do
it first. Set the point temperature fairly
low. All you have to do is produce a
rather long flick stroke. Hold the point on
the wood where you traced the tip of one
of the antennae for a fraction of a second,
and then pull the line in towards the
head. Then do the same for the other.
Perhaps the best way to describe the
result you are aiming for is an ear of
wheat in reverse. You must be confident
and positive when attempting effects of
this sort, and try to get them right first
time. A line like this is very difficult to go
over a second time, and in fact this should
not be necessary if the line is made
positively and confidently in the first
place. Again, some practice on a spare
scrap of similar wood is a good idea.

Outline and vein lines

Use a similar temperature setting to the
one you used for the antennae. You will
need to use a fair amount of pressure, but
at the same time be sure of burning the
trace lines out completely. To be accurate

you also need to work slowly. Remember to have a scrap of wood handy to test the point on (*see* page 25). This, incidentally, is a rule you should always observe.

Start working on the outside of the butterfly's wings, and try to start and finish each line in one go. When the outer edges of the wings are pyrographed, put in the lines that will represent the veins. These need to be fairly deeply pushed into the wood, so use the side of the wire point (*see* Fig 8.3). In this position the point is at its strongest and is least likely to bend. If the point does bend slightly, turn it round and press it against a scrap of wood until it is back in its correct position. The wire for making the points is very pliable, and will stand up quite readily to this treatment.

With the outline and the veins of the butterfly completed, carefully burn in the traced lines of the body (or thorax) and two dots for the eyes, and you are ready for the next stage. This will require the use of the spoon point.

Wings

Again, it is very important to try out the effects you are hoping to obtain on a scrap of wood. The object of the next stage is to fill in the wings with a tone or texture that corresponds to the soft texture of a real butterfly wing. Set the temperature of the spoon point so that with a little pressure a dark line can be formed. You will soon know if the setting is too high because some 'overburning' will occur (*see* page 29). You will need to work slowly for accuracy, so keep the temperature down. When you are happy that the temperature setting is correct, see if you can produce a small area of tone starting from dark at the top to light at the bottom. Stroke the spoon point across the wood in short lines side by side to cover an area about the size of the wing. Now do the same on the butterfly itself. Work from the outside of the wing towards the body of the butterfly but stopping short of actually reaching the body. Make your shading lines follow the direction of the vein lines. The spoon point will be at its hottest when first in contact with the wood, but will cool slightly as you are using it. If done properly this should give a wonderful soft shading effect (*see* Fig 8.4). When you have come to the end of the

Fig 8.4
Shading the wings with the spoon point.

Fig 8.5
Flick stroking the hairs on the body.

outer wing edge, repeat the process carefully in the other direction, working from the body outwards. Do not worry about going over the vein lines; if you pyrographed them deeply enough it will be impossible for the spoon point to obliterate them. Now repeat the process with the other wing. When completed, the shading gives an almost three-dimensional appearance to the butterfly wings.

Body

The butterfly is not intended to be any particular species, so there is scope to borrow interesting features from a number of species. For example, many butterflies have quite hairy bodies. The small tortoiseshell is one that particularly comes to mind. This is a very interesting texture to try to reproduce, and a good

example of how pyrography can have an edge over other mediums. First gently shade in the body area with the spoon. The temperature setting you are already using should be adequate for this. From an imaginary line running down the centre of the body, and working from the centre of the body outwards, make some flick strokes with the edge of the spoon point. A bit of practice first on a scrap of wood will help. These flick strokes should suggest the hairs on the body of your butterfly (*see* Fig 8.5). The sharp edge of the spoon point will in effect cut into the wood surface, and where it is done over existing burning it will cut through it. That is why it can only be done at this stage and not earlier.

This tracing exercise and simple composition should now be complete.

CHAPTER 9

Producing Lifelike Textures

The projects in this chapter are designed to further develop your skills in the pyrographic reproduction of tones and textures found in nature. In the course of producing a mouse and a blackberry design, you will learn how to represent in a very realistic fashion the look and texture of natural features such as fur, skin, eyes, leaves, berries, stalks and stems.

Fig 9.1
Mouse template.

Fig 9.2
The mouse transferred on to the wood.

Mouse

For this exercise you will need to make a photocopy of the 'mouse' plan (*see* Fig 9.1). You will notice that there are no actual lines to trace other than those that represent the ears, eyes and paws. In fact there is very little detail at all. The dots are all directional guide marks to show where your pyrographed lines begin and which direction they travel. This exercise has a dual purpose: firstly it will show you how to make a pyrograph almost entirely by the use of texture, and secondly it will show how any illustration or photograph (especially where wildlife subjects are concerned) can be transferred in the form of a plan onto a wood surface.

The template (*see* Fig 9.1) is representative of the maximum numbers of lines and marks you would need when tracing from an original or from a photocopy of an original picture of a similar subject. In other words, these lines and marks are simply clues for you to follow with the pyrography pencil; they will all be eventually burnt away. The more carbon marks and pencil lines there are, the harder it is to dispose of them. When you have traced a minimum of marks onto the wood (*see* Fig 9.2), you can concentrate on the detail by referring to the original picture, secure in the knowledge that you already have the proportions of the subject correct.

Tracing the mouse

Trace the details from the template onto your wood surface as with the butterfly exercise (*see* Chapter 8). Ensure that you trace precisely what is there, and that where the marks are directional, yours are the same. Take particular care to press gently, making very light marks with the carbon. The outline of the eyes is particularly important; as is usual with a life subject or portrait, the viewer's eyes will focus on the eyes of the subject, and if they are wrong it will be the first thing that is noticed. Do not add any detail you think should be there; remember that this is only a working plan. When you are satisfied that the template has been fully traced, remove it and attach it further up the wood where it can be referred to if need be.

Used pencil carbon paper is not always a faithful intermediary in the tracing process (it may have been used unevenly on the typewriter) and you may have parts of your tracing that are rather darker than they should be. If this has happened, you can tone down the offending areas by sanding them gently with a piece of very worn sandpaper (or else rub two pieces of sandpaper together

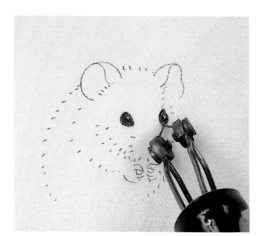

Fig 9.3

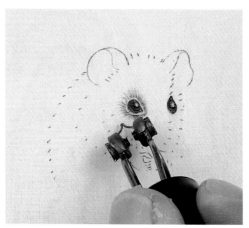

Fig 9.4

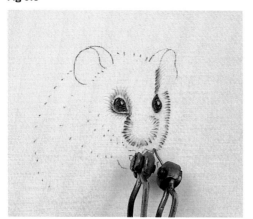

Fig 9.5

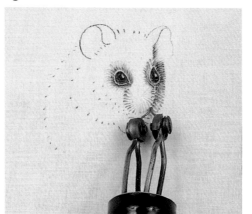

Fig 9.6

Fig 9.3
Burning in the eyes.
Fig 9.4
Short flick strokes are inserted around the left eye to suggest the eye is slightly recessed within the head.
Fig 9.5
Flick stroking the fur marks delineating the edge of the mouse's face.
Fig 9.6
The right eye now completed, further work is done on developing the texture on the side of the face.

to reduce their abrasiveness and use one of them). A pencil rubber will remove some of the carbon, but some smudging will probably result. If the sandpaper removes any fine detail, this can be restored with a soft pencil, using the template as a guide.

Eyes

The eyes are a tricky area, and therefore best dealt with first. Another reason for starting here is that the mouse is going to be formed by working on different areas at a time, and will look a little strange until near completion. Working on the eyes first will help it to look more like the intended subject earlier.

Set the point to a very low temperature. You want to form a dark area for the eyes, and for the sake of accuracy you must work slowly.

Carefully pyrograph the outline of the eyes first, then leaving a tiny area within each eye to represent the highlights, burn the eyes in as darkly as possible (*see* Fig 9.3).

The next stages are done with a lot of importance placed on texture. It does not matter at this stage how light the pyrographed lines are. In fact you could create a lot of fur texture with the transformer switched off. Once the grooves are in the wood, it is an easy task to darken them by going over them either more slowly, or by slightly increasing the temperature. If, on the other hand, you make the lines dark to begin with, it is very difficult to lighten them.

Bearing this in mind, and again with a very low temperature setting, put a series of short, slightly curved flick strokes around the left eye (as you are facing the mouse) (*see* Fig 9.4). Make sure that each mark starts a little bit away from the actual eye, and that the flick stroke is what the word suggests and not a short line. You will be making many of these types of mark, and if they are not done properly you will create a lot of extra lines that you do not want, formed by the ends of marks. Study Fig 9.4 carefully to make sure the direction of your marks is correct. The two different textures of the actual eye and the surround will give the impression that the eye is in a socket and has not just been stuck on the mouse's head.

Before working on the other eye it is necessary to do some work around it first. You will see a row of marks running from the top of the right eye to the base of the ear. Working in an outward direction, flick-stroke these in, and then do similarly with the marks that appear down the side of the face, only in this instance work inwards (*see* Fig 9.5). All the marks representing fur lines must be pyrographed inwards. Again this is to prevent the formation of double lines. Finally, pyrograph the marks that represent the mouse's face. Now you are ready to put in the texture of the other eye. Again, working from a point just short of the actual eye, pyrograph a series of short lines with a little more pressure,

working from the eyeball outwards as with the left eye. These lines and this texture will form the side of the face (*see* Fig 9.6). With these first stages completed, the mouse should be starting to come to life.

Outline

Working from the outside, pyrograph all the remaining trace marks in a similar manner to the previous ones (*see* Fig 9.7). Keep religiously to the direction of the marks, and fill in the gaps between each mark with additional marks. It doesn't really matter how many extra little marks you pyrograph in; what is important is that you keep them in a neat line around the body of the mouse, so his fur doesn't appear ruffled, and even more important, so that all the carbon trace lines are burnt away.

Slightly increasing the temperature, burn in the outline of the ears and paws. You are now ready to put in the main areas of texture.

Texture

Starting at the top of the mouse's head, pyrograph slightly longer lines in the direction shown in Fig 9.8. These are just longer 'flick' strokes really; make sure they do not have ends or blobs. Continue with this texture, working your way to the bottom of the mouse's face. The lines should appear to 'funnel' down between the eyes. Again it is the texture that is important; do not worry if the lines are not a dark colour at this stage. Carry on working the lines from the base of the left ear.

The next stage, if executed correctly, will put to advantage the double-line effect that until now you have been trying to avoid. Link up the marks that show the left cheek with the marks that were pyrographed earlier around the left eye, using a curved line to emphasize the roundness of the face. Repeat the process, this time from the marks that represent the top of the forearm (using a touch more heat), but continue each pyrographed line right through the one above. This will

Fig 9.7
Pyrographing the remaining trace marks.

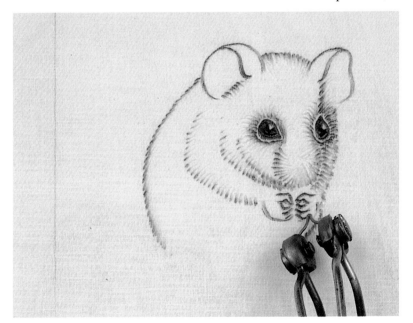

Fig 9.8
Putting in the texture of the mouse's fur.

Fig 9.9
The fur lines are darkened to enhance the overall look and texture of the mouse.

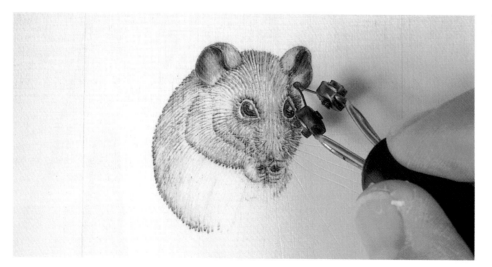

Fig 9.10
Working on the mouse's ears.

give a very subtle double-line effect, perfect for showing how the fur lines between arm and face are formed. Repeat the process a third time from the bottom of the arm, again passing the point right through to meet the texture at the bottom of the eye.

Although you may not have a very dark mouse at this stage, if you shine your work lamp across the work you have completed so far, you should see a definite furry texture. To complete this stage, treat the back as shown in Fig 9.8, maintaining a slight curve to each pyrographed line and increasing the arc as you get nearer to the part below the paws.

The basics are now done; if you have followed the steps correctly, the remaining part of the exercise should not pose any problems. To increase the three-dimensional effect of this multi-grooved texture, it is necessary to work further on some of the areas already pyrographed in order to darken them. To do this, combine a slight increase in temperature with a slower more deliberate working over these areas (*see* Fig 9.9). The parts that need to be made darker are:

- From the top of the head, down through to the front of the face.
- The right-hand side of the face.
- The back, especially from a point starting behind the left ear where you would expect to see a darker area.
- Behind the paws.

The more you work on this particular illustration, the more believable it becomes. To continue going over and over the fur texture almost seems to groom the fur. Patience is well repaid. I have found when I hurry this project I finish up with a mouse that looks as though he has just come out of the shower and shaken his fur to dry himself.

Ears and whiskers

To complete the mouse, some texture needs to be added to the ears. The outer

parts can simply be carefully shaded in with the point. Use very little pressure and a low temperature setting. It is important to differentiate between the furry texture of the mouse's body, and the soft skin-like surface of the ear. Make your strokes from the top to the bottom of the area as uniform as you can. The inner part is much darker as you would expect of an area in shadow. This requires the spoon point. The idea is to produce a small dark area without pressing too hard and thereby creating unwanted texture. You must work very slowly with a low temperature setting to achieve this. As you work carefully towards the outer edge of the ear, gradually decrease the pressure whilst slightly increasing your speed. This will cause a graduated paling of the dark shaded area and suggest depth (*see* Fig 9.10).

You may like to give your mouse a few whiskers. The best way to do this is to use a point at the lowest possible setting. Working from the face outwards, make a few rapid cuts, sweeping away from the face. This will give an impression of long fine whiskers. The effect is caused by the minute shadow created by light passing across the cut marks rather than by any burning.

Fig 9.11
Blackberry panel template.

🔲 Blackberry panel design

I would tend to use this type of design on a box lid or even a plaque that could be used as a key holder. The project illustrated in Figs 9.11 to 9.18 was executed on a plaque of kiln-dried sycamore measuring 9/16 x 7 x 10in (14 x 178 x 254mm), and supplied by Janik.

Tracing the design

Photocopy Fig 9.11 to the size required.

Fig 9.12 (right)
The completed tracing.
Fig 9.13 (far right)
The outlines, including the thorns, partially pyrographed.

Cut down the photocopy to a size slightly less than the area of the wood surface, position it and attach it on one side with masking tape. Carefully trace through using the black carbon paper with a very hard (4H), sharp pencil (*see* Fig 9.12). Check after you have made the initial marks that you are not pressing too hard or too lightly with the pencil. It is a good idea to check this regularly as it is easy to press harder and harder as the tracing progresses and the pencil begins to lose its fine point. This in turn produces too thick a trace line which is difficult to burn away. There is no need to spend a lot of time on the detail of the thorns at this stage: just marking their position will suffice.

When you consider the tracing complete, before removing the photocopy lift it from the surface and back a few times very quickly; anything missed out can usually be detected by this method. When you are satisfied that everything is in place, remove the plan (*see* Fig 9.12). You may find that despite all your care the tracing is still too bold in places. This can be rectified by gently applying a pencil rubber which will pick up the excess carbon on its surface. (It helps to have a clean piece of paper handy to clean the rubber with and therefore prevent any smudging.) Should you, on the other hand, find that odd bits of detail are either faint or missing, use the plan to pencil them in with a soft (2B) pencil.

Outline

Using the wire point you can now make a start by burning away the traced outline (*see* Fig 9.13). You might like to make the edges of the leaves more realistic at this stage by defining them more accurately. Set the temperature in a way that will allow you to engrave at a reasonable speed without causing any overburning or singeing of the wood around the trace lines. The best way to do this is to set the temperature to an average (*see* page 27). Remember, have a spare piece of similar wood handy to test that it is set correctly.

Try to make sure that none of the trace lines are visible after pyrographing the outline – it will be more difficult to disguise them at a later stage. With a piece of work like this you will find it helps to turn the wood as you work

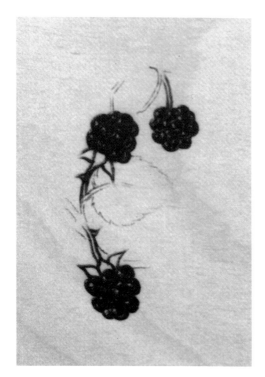

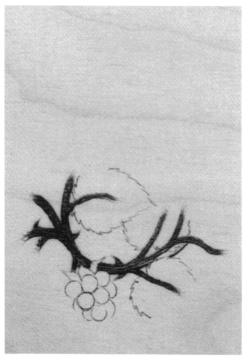

Fig 9.14 (far left)
Some berry segments.
Fig 9.15 (left)
Aim for a rough, woody texture for the stalks and stems.

instead of having it set in the same position all the time. At a slightly lower temperature, to ensure accuracy, burn in the thorn outlines; two short curved flick strokes from the stem that meet to form a sharp point. Push fairly hard at the beginning of the stroke to ensure the thorn has a fat base. By varying pressure and speed the size of the thorn can be altered. It is always a good idea to practise this several times on your test piece first.

Berries

With all traces of traced carbon removed you can now start to work on the berries. Turn the temperature down still further. Remember: to obtain the blackest of marks you need a low temperature worked slowly with enough pressure not to bend the point. You also need to use the rounded end of the point instead of angling it to the surface; this will minimize the forming of any unwanted texture on what is essentially a smooth, round subject. The more patience you can summon and the more slowly you work, the blacker the result. The berry segments

can be treated in an identical way to the eyes of the mouse (*see* page 62). Leaving a small space for a highlight (and making sure it appears in the same area of each segment), burn in a circular movement, slowly, with a low temperature setting, and some pressure (*see* Fig 9.14). Continue until all the berries have been pyrographed.

Stalks, stems and leaves

The next task is to fill in the stalks and stems. The stems of a blackberry have a rather rough, woody texture and you want to try and show this. This is a relatively simple task requiring slightly more temperature from the point than with the berries, more speed, and as much pressure using the side of the point as you can manage (*see* Fig 9.15).

The small leaves directly at the base of the berry, by contrast to the stems, are of a soft texture, similar to the mouse's ear (*see* page 65). These little areas can be shaded using the wire point at a fairly low temperature setting, and with very little pressure. Work from the base of the berry on each of these tiny areas in uniform

Fig 9.16 (right)
The small leaves at the base of the berries should have a soft texture.

Fig 9.17 (far right)
Some leaves partially completed, showing the dimensional effect obtained by the darker area at the start of each line of shading, and by the placing of some of the leaves in shadow.

strokes. This will produce a darker shading effect just where you want it, showing the natural shadow caused by the leaf coming from under the berry (*see* Fig 9.16).

The final stages need a lot of care, particularly with the temperature setting of the spoon. It is very important to get everything set correctly and tested on your piece of scrap wood before proceeding. Working from the base of the leaf and from the line you engraved through the centre, use the same technique employed when producing the dark areas inside the ear of the mouse (*see* page 65). You need to work quite slowly at an average heat setting, using as much pressure as you can without actually bending the spoon point. As each broad line is pyrographed deeply into the wood surface, a raised edge will form between each line, giving a suggestion of veins in the leaves. Also be aware that the leaves will not all be the same density of colour; some will be tucked behind in a shadow area and can be quite dark. Trace one or two leaves from your photocopy onto the test wood so you can practise properly

before working on the actual piece. Always work from the centre of the leaf outwards. The darker area that is formed at the beginning of each mark will add some dimension to the leaf (*see* Fig 9.17).

Final touches

As a final step, when all the leaves have been pyrographed, sit back and study your work for awhile making sure nothing has been missed out. With a rather complicated design like this it is easy to miss a small section of stem or maybe a thorn. You may like to consider increasing some of the shading with the spoon point where leaves overlap and would form very positive shadows. Maybe an extra thorn or two might balance a slightly weak or open section of the design.

The only decision left to make is whether the finished piece of pyrography is to be varnished or polished, and whether it is to become a practical object or simply a piece of work to be mounted and admired.

Fig 9.18
The completed blackberry
panel.

CHAPTER 10

Shading Techniques

The project in this chapter is a hinge design, and it has been chosen as a means of demonstrating how a quite ordinary design can be enhanced by the introduction of shadows and graduated shading, using both wire and spoon points. The resulting design can be used to decorate a box lid or, alternatively, a simpler version could provide a decoration for a small picture frame or be used as a repeat pattern for a border.

■ The source of the design

It may be of interest to readers to know how this design originated. I am always on the lookout for old craft books. Most of the books published from the 1930s to the 1950s are out of date as far as equipment is concerned, but there are often plenty of illustrations and line drawings that can be adapted for pyrographic purposes.

The flower in the centre of the design came from a section in a pre-war craft book dealing with the manufacture of paper flowers. The designs on either side of the flower have been adapted from a drawing suggesting a design for an elaborate metal hinge. All I have done is redraw the hinge, leaving out the screw fittings, and slightly exaggerating the overlapping parts of the design. As you will appreciate, the original would have been a flat metal cut-out. By tracing my finished line drawing and then reversing it, I have produced the mirror image of the same design for the other side.

■ The project

This is intended as an exercise, so the design has been produced reasonably large at approximately 9½in (241mm) in length. Obviously the smaller the design is the harder it is to pyrograph, and the less detail is possible. A standard Janik sycamore plaque of 12¾ x 8¾in (324 x 222mm) has been used in the photographs, but it is advisable to try this first on a piece of birch-faced plywood.

Pyrographing the lines

Trace your design through the carbon paper in the usual way. Do not worry too much about producing a dark tracing this time; the lines you need to burn out will be fairly thick. Take care to keep these initial burnings uniform. Set the point to a temperature that allows you to produce a black line slowly and with some pressure. If the point is too hot you will either have to work too quickly, or run the risk of overburning (*see* pages 29–30). You should aim to produce a crisp, solid dark line. Another small but important point to remember is to avoid working entirely from one side of the design to the other. Complete a section on one side, then

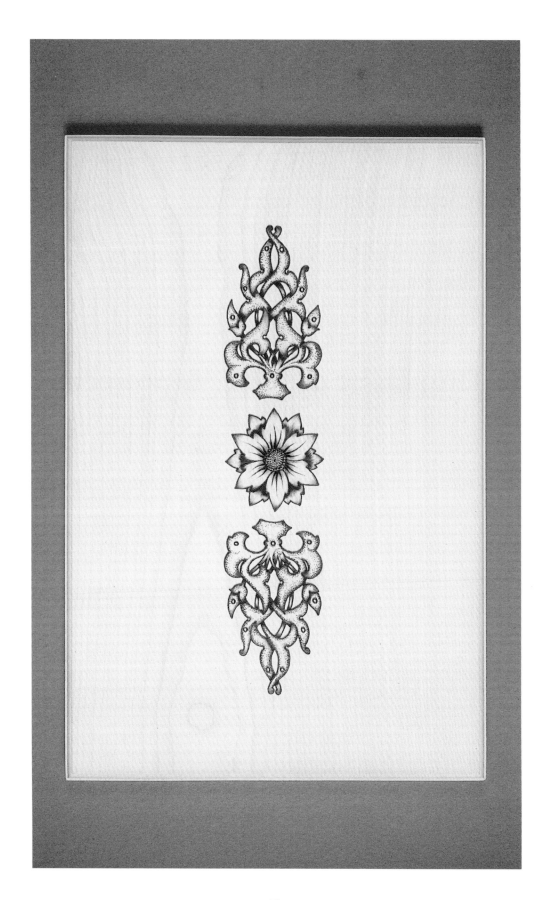

Fig 10.1
Hinge template.

complete the equivalent section on the other side. This is to ensure that symmetry and continuity are maintained (*see* Fig 10.2). Always test the point on a scrap of similar material to the one you are working on, and periodically recheck it before applying the heat to the wood. Finally, make absolutely certain that you do not trip yourself up early on by putting a line where one should not be. With any complex work like this, where there are a host of lines over- and under-lapping, a line in the wrong place burned deeply could pose a big problem. Should you make this kind of error, you can gently scrape away the mistake with the point of a 10A scalpel blade and then carefully sand the area affected with a tiny piece of sandpaper. However, it is obviously preferable not to make the mistake in the first place. You should now have a nicely engraved line drawing of the original design (*see* Fig 10.3).

Shading

The next stages require the use of the spoon point. The temperature setting is critical for this first part, and it is worth spending some time getting it right. With practice it will become automatic as you grow more familiar with your machine. Turn the temperature to a very low setting so that the spoon must rest on the wood for a second or two before the heat marks it. A very slight increase in temperature from this setting is likely to be the one you need.

Using a minimum of pressure, and working carefully and slowly with a stroking movement, shade in the points of the design (*see* Fig 10.4). Begin at the points within the outer designs, gradually reducing the pressure at the end of each stroke. You are trying to create the effect of a graduated tint running from dark to light. As you did earlier, work on an area on one side and then repeat the work on the equivalent area on the other side, before returning to the original side to work on a new area. When you have finished shading in these points, carry out

Fig 10.2 (far left)
Pyrographing the lines. Aim for a crisp, solid, dark line, swapping sides as you go, rather than progressing from one side to the other.
Fig 10.3 (left)
The lines fully engraved.

Fig 10.4 (right)
The points of the design shaded in.
Fig 10.5 (far right)
The points of the flower shaded in.

Fig 10.6 (far left)
The lines on the petals of the flower are achieved by overburning with the spoon point.
Fig 10.7 (left)
The shadows on the hinge and the flower shaded in.

Fig 10.8
A close-up of the flower showing the 'C' shaped marks that make up its centre burned in.

the same process on the points of the flower petals in the centre of the design (*see* Fig 10.5).

The next stage is a test of your skill in temperature setting. First heat the spoon point until it is literally red hot. To do this, turn the control dial slowly, not fast, watching the point until it has a slight glow. The idea now is to mark in the lines that are formed from the centre of the flower. Practise this a little first. When you feel confident, push the end of the spoon point into the wood and then draw it away from the starting point in a fairly swift cutting movement. If the heat is right for this you will probably actually hear it burn the surface. The overburning that you avoided when you were burning in the outline is what you are aiming for here. This may sound difficult, but with a little practice and courage these positive marks can be achieved (*see* Fig 10.6). This is the only part of the design that you need to treat in this way and, admittedly, would normally be left until later, but it is

important that you learn how to change from one temperature setting to another and back with confidence.

Now go back to the hinge part of the design and study it carefully for a few moments. If you begin on the left-hand side, use the spoon point to carefully shade all the little areas that appear to be emerging from beneath other areas. There will be many times that you will have to do this with all kinds of pyrography and the practice gained from this exercise is time well spent. The flower can receive similar treatment; in order to draw attention to it I have deliberately over-darkened the petals at the back (*see* Fig 10.7). It is up to you whether you follow suit.

Using the wire point

Now you are very nearly there. The centre of the flower is a job for the ordinary wire point, so again, unless you have the luxury of two pyrography pencils, you

Fig 10.9
The completed design,
including the graduated dot
effect on the hinge area.

will have to swap the points. Whether you have purchased your spoons or made them yourself, do not necessarily discard a used one when you have finished with it. A spoon point that has been used for a while and you have become accustomed to can be employed again and again.

The whole area of the flower's centre is made up of tiny 'C' shaped marks (*see* Fig 10.8). To do this, the point needs to be set at a slightly lower temperature to the one that was used to produce the original outline. Mark in a series of 'C' marks two lines deep around the outer edge, gradually reducing the pressure as you work towards the middle. Create one more heavily burned 'C' shape in the centre, and the job is done.

You may be satisfied to leave the design at this stage, but there is one more item that can be added if you wish. Using the wire point set at the temperature you used at the start for the outlines, continue with a series of dots, working from the darker shaded areas inwards (*see* Fig 10.9). As you move towards the otherwise untouched parts of each segment, reduce the pressure and increase your working speed until you are working too fast for the point to actually burn the wood. You will need to have the pencil almost upright at this stage to ensure that you are using the tip of the point only. This is a little tedious to do, but it is another form of shading and another useful effect to add to your growing repertoire.

CHAPTER 11

Colour in Pyrography

Adding colour to a pyrograph is not a new idea, and there are plenty of examples of coloured pyrography to be found on display at craft fairs, craft shops, art centres and so forth. Unfortunately, most of the examples I have come across tend to show a minimal appreciation of the skills of the pyrographer, essentially comprising a burnt outline that has simply been coloured in.

This is fine as far as it goes and, to be fair, it is a relatively straightforward and often very effective way of reproducing multiples of popular pieces of craftwork. But it is not pyrography, and if you have worked your way through this book and handled the tasks that have been set, I am sure you will be reluctant to demean your new skills by being content to produce nothing more than coloured-in burnt outlines. Personally I feel that colour should never take over the pyrograph. In other words, it is better to aim for a pyrograph enhanced by the careful use of colour, than to produce a painting with some pyrography.

Methods of colouring

When applying colour to a pyrograph, the first concern is for the textures already produced on the wood surface. It would be unfortunate if they were to be obscured by solid areas of pigment. In order to preserve the look of the pyrograph, it is best to use a water-soluble paint, and of these I recommend gouache. This possesses a stronger and denser pigment than watercolour, but can be diluted with water to the thinnest of applications without losing its colour strength in the way that watercolour appears to. Gouache was extensively used by graphic designers at one time for producing visuals and often finished designs. It is also used by artists specializing in wildlife-type illustrations, again because of its positive colour

properties. Watercolour – and indeed acrylic paints – can be used to add dimension to a piece of pyrography, but I have yet to find anything I prefer to gouache.

As already stated, the idea is not to obscure skillfully produced texture, but to enhance it. For example, it would be undesirable for the wing of a butterfly, carefully pyrographed to create the effect of the veins, to be covered with a thick coat of colour. Use the colour sparingly with plenty of water to thin the pigment when you are mixing; you can build the colour up with additional coats to the required density. You will discover that heavily pyrographed areas of wood, particularly where the spoon point has been used, will not readily accept the paint. It is therefore suggested that areas you are planning to colour, especially large areas, should not be too heavily pyrographed. This will make them more paint receptive without the problem of

Fig 11.1
A feathery texture was
pyrographed before adding
colour to this kingfisher in
order to produce a more
lifelike effect.

Fig 11.2
My version of an 18th century engraving of Newmarket Races. In this piece, pyrographed on a solid sycamore block, only one dye was used in varying densities to achieve the desired effect.

the paint having nothing to key into.

It is possible nowadays to buy wood dye in a variety of colours, but be careful. The dye is absorbed by the wood very much faster than water-based paints or paints thinned by water. The reason for this is that wood dyes are generally spirit or solvent based, and are designed to soak into the material being dyed. However, in the case of watercolours, or any paint thinned with water, the pigment tends to sit on the surface, while the water soaks into the material. Dye can be used to good effect but it needs to be used with care and very sparingly, preferably with a small sable brush. (The best way to do this is to load the brush and then paint with it on a spare piece of wood similar to the one upon which you are working, until it ceases to streak out of control.) You may be surprised at how little you need. The density of colour can be increased by applying additional coats. An example of this technique can be seen in Fig 11.2. An additional safeguard is to ensure that as many of the areas to be dyed are enclosed and protected by positively engraved lines or solid areas. This will impede the running of the dye and is a case where the colouring-in approach mentioned earlier is justified.

Where you are adding colour to an area that is a combination of heavily pyrographed marks, and heavily pyrographed marks with little or no heat – for example, our old friend the mouse (*see* Chapter 9) – you will need to use a stronger or more concentrated colour, the density of which will be reduced on contact with the combination of minute areas that are non-receptive to the paint, and the minute areas of bare, unpyrographed wood. If you think about it – and even better if you study the results of your labours under a magnifying glass – you will see that the final impression of colour is composed of a range of things: the dark and light of the pyrography, the colour of the bare wood, and the colour of the paint you have added. The texture, undiminished by the addition of colour, will still give the impression of an extra dimension unachievable by simply adding paint to paper or wood. The only way the watercolour artist can get anywhere near to achieving this, is to work on a heavily textured or embossed paper; in other words, to cheat.

Colouring project: three butterflies

This project includes a simple introduction to colouring a pyrograph. Its purpose is also to show by stages how three similar designs treated in different ways will give contrasting results. You will need a piece of sycamore 7 x 10in (178 x 254mm) or similar. Trace a photocopy of Fig 11.3 on to the wood surface using the method described in Chapter 8. However, with the butterfly on the right, use a pencil rubber after tracing to remove as much as possible of the carbon so that you end up with the minimum of carbon on the wood surface.

Burning the carbon outline away

The first stage of this project, as usual, is to burn the carbon outline away (*see* Fig 11.4). Start with the butterfly in the centre; use a reasonable amount of pressure and work slowly. The idea is to produce a dark and solid line. When this task has been completed, move to the butterfly on the left and do the same. For this one use a little less heat and pressure, but be aware that a fairly deep mark in the wood will enhance the work and make the veins in the wings appear more realistic. Finally, move to the butterfly on the extreme right. This is the one that will

Fig 11.3
Three butterflies template.

have colour added so it is less important to produce a dark line, though vitally important to form a deep one. To do this, turn the temperature very low and use the maximum pressure. Position the point on its side when you use it, to give it more strength and prevent it from bending too easily.

Butterfly One

You will have guessed by now that the intention is to produce a dark, solid butterfly in the centre. Use the spoon point for this stage. The temperature setting is fairly critical so a little practice on the ever-present piece of scrap wood may be required. What you are aiming for is a dark stroke that gradually decreases in strength as you sweep towards the centre of the butterfly (*see* Fig 11.5). The temperature of the spoon does not need to be too high, but high enough to give you the dark burn you need without

exerting too much pressure. The temperature of the metal will be at its highest the moment you actually touch the wood with it, cooling immediately on contact. To avoid any overburning when you make the first contact, you may find it helpful to gently blow onto the spoon.

When you have finished working around the outer edge, apply a similar technique to the inside edge. With a smaller area to cover you will need to reduce the temperature a little to allow for the shorter strokes you will be making. Start each mark from the outer edge of the body.

To complete the body, shade in the abdomen with the spoon point, slowing down the strokes slightly beneath the stripes to give a shaded area effect. After shading in the upper abdomen, the final touch is to suggest the fine hairs normally seen on this type of insect. At a still lower temperature, use the edge of the spoon to produce at speed a series of cuts working

Fig 11.4
The outlines pyrographed.

Fig 11.5
Butterfly One's wings
shaded at the outer edge.

Fig 11.6
The inner parts of the wings
shaded, and the body
pyrographed.

Fig 11.7
Butterfly Two's wings and
body shaded.

from the line in the centre outwards (*see* Fig 11.6). Make sure you practise this effect first; it is easy to ruin the work by being overeager and careless.

Butterfly Two

Now you can move on to the butterfly on the left. Begin by repeating the shading technique you used on the first butterfly, only at a much lower temperature. At this lower temperature, and using less pressure, you will notice more clearly that the spoon glides over the deep lines of the veins in the wings making them appear to stand out. A simple test is to lay a piece of greaseproof paper on the pyrography, and then, with the side of the lead of a soft pencil, gently pencil over the butterfly. If you have got the correct result the detail of the deeply pyrographed lines should be clearly visible (*see* Fig 11.7). The body of the butterfly can be completed as before (*see* page 85).

The butterflies in this project do not exist as a species; they have been created by me for the purpose of instruction and demonstration. However, many actual species of butterfly are adorned with varied and beautiful patterns, often for reasons of camouflage or identification by other butterflies of the same species. These patterns are not that difficult to emulate pyrographically, and the following stage is designed to show you how.

Mark in with a soft pencil a few lines for guidance. You can copy the pattern in Fig 11.8, or just invent your own. However, try and ensure that the designs on the wings are symmetrical. When you have a reasonable selection of lines, burn them in and remove any unused lines with the pencil rubber. Ideally, the type of line you need is similar to the outline on the butterfly in the centre. Remember: not too much temperature or speed, just a solid, dark, positive line. Allow the lines to taper or fade a little at the ends.

Now change back to the spoon, and, working from the line towards the middle of the butterfly at a low temperature setting, gently shade in with a stroking movement. Practise this on a scrap piece of wood first until you are confident. If you can do this properly, the effect is quite stunning and demonstrates how burning wood with hot metal can produce the subtlest of work (*see* Fig 11.9).

Fig 11.8
The markings burned on to the wings with the wire point.

Fig 11.9
Further shading work carried out on the markings, this time with the spoon point.

Fig 11.10
The wings of Butterfly Three coloured with yellow designer's gouache slightly diluted with water.

Fig 11.11
The application of a complementary dark green colour as a thick line at the edge of the upper and lower wings; the right-hand wings show the effect to aim for when working the green into the yellow 'undercoat'.

Fig 11.12
The body of Butterfly Three pyrographed.

Fig 11.13
Optional extra patterns that can be applied to the wings of Butterfly Three.

Butterfly Three: the application of colour

You may now turn your attention to the remaining outlined butterfly on the right. In this example I have used designer's gouache. Select a light colour such as white (permanent) or yellow. Using a small sable brush (a no. 1 is suitable for most colouring work of this size) and some paint slightly diluted with water, carefully colour in the wings of the butterfly. Normally you would expect the paint to spread out of control over the wood and over the outline you have pyrographed. This will not happen if the pyrographed lines are deep, and the paint is not too watered down. The paint will not readily adhere to the lines of the veins, but do persevere with this. Allow the paint to dry, which will take about five minutes, then apply a second coat. The idea is to build up a fairly thick coating (see Fig 11.10).

For the next stage, choose a darker colour that will complement the original colour. Carefully apply a thick line as shown in Fig 11.11 on the upper and lower left wings. Try as hard as you can to work from the very edge and be sure that none of the first colour is showing. For the next, more difficult stage, make sure your brush is clean and be prepared to frequently clean the colour from it. To achieve the effect shown in Fig 11.11 you need to gently work the darker colour into the lighter colour. You will only need the brush to be damp for this, as though you have wetted it in your mouth (although I am not suggesting you actually do this). This whole process needs to be carried out carefully and slowly. Too much moisture or pressure and you will remove too much of the 'undercoat'. Repeat the process on the opposing two wings. The body of the butterfly can now be completed as before (see page 85 and Fig 11.12).

You might like to experiment further with this process by adding a few more dark lines and painting some additional patterns on the butterfly in the second colour (see Fig 11.13) along the lines of the pyrography patterns made on Butterfly Two.

This project is a useful starting point for anyone who wishes to experiment with the possibilities of combining colour with pyrography. As well as gouache, coloured wood dyes can be used. Also, gentle washes and tints can be applied to give a background colour to a wood surface before beginning a pyrograph.

Colouring project: cockerel

I have already stated my aversion to the overapplication of colour in pyrography; if your intention is to produce a pyrograph, then too much colour will detract from the real purpose of the work. However, it must be said that pyrographic skills can be used to good effect when combined with a painting on wood. In this project, the pyrography is used merely to create textures that will enhance the detail of the work, introducing the hint of an additional dimension.

Fig 11.14
Cockerel template.

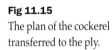

Fig 11.15
The plan of the cockerel
transferred to the ply.

Pyrographing the outline

The plan of the bird is laid down onto the wood surface (*see* Figs 11.14 and 11.15). For this project I have used a piece of finely sanded birch-faced plywood. It will help with the painting of fine detail if the wood is very well sanded, and therefore extremely smooth, since the bird is to be painted with designer's gouache. The temperature of the wire point needs to be hot enough to produce a clear burn working at slow speed. You will need to work slowly, applying as much pressure as you can in order to make as deep an

engraved line as possible (*see* Fig 11.16). The drawing is really a plan of the feather formations.

Texturing

Once all the outlines have been pyrographed in, your attention can be turned to producing the textures. I have concentrated my own efforts on the wing and tail feathers, as these are the areas that will benefit most from this technique. The marks you now make must be positive enough to show through the painting to come, and while you are producing these marks try to imagine what the effect of the colour will be.

The breast of the bird does not enjoy much variation of tone; however, you will notice the series of 'V' shaped marks in pencil (*see* Fig 11.16). Use the wire point to push some fairly deep gouges in a series of lines working from the bottom upwards (*see* Fig 11.17). The colour of the breast is going to be dark, so you will not see very much texture; nevertheless it is a good and easy place to start. The wire point can also be used on what will be the little white tuft at the base of the tail feathers, and on the area at the rear end of

the bird, tucked behind the wing feathers, that appears in shadow. Push the point into the surface as hard as you can in these areas; you may have to apply several coats of paint on top of them, so a certain amount of filling in might take place (*see* Fig 11.17).

A couple of small areas that need a little work with the wire point are the comb of the bird and the tiny area of the head where the feathers appear from behind the comb. Those of you who have seen close up a cockerel's or chicken's comb will know that it is a rather pitted flap of loose skin. Push a heated point in a

Fig 11.16
The lines of the plan should be pyrographed as deeply as possible. Note 'V' shaped marks on chest.

Fig 11.17
The wire point is used to texture the chest area, the little white tuft at the base of the tail feathers, and the rear of the bird beneath the wing feathers.

series of dots into the comb to help give it that look. Then, using the edge of the end of the point, cut in some fine shadow lines and texture lines to show the fine feathers coming from behind the comb.

It is time to turn to the spoon point. This is without doubt the best tool for creating deep pyrographed lines that are to be painted. Use the cutting edge of the spoon with sufficient temperature to help the point into the wood, then pyrograph a series of deeply cut lines to represent the texture of the feathers. This effect is best seen on the larger main tail feathers (*see* Fig 11.18). Remember to try and make

these cuts as deep as possible.

Painting

I do not profess to be a painter, and that is not what this book is about. However, on the more specialized subject of painting with gouache on wood pre-treated with a pyrographed texture, I am quite happy to pass on my own discoveries and talk about the methods I used.

Despite the density of pigment in gouache, it is a good idea to prepare the work with an undercoat, especially where the lighter colours are involved. For this

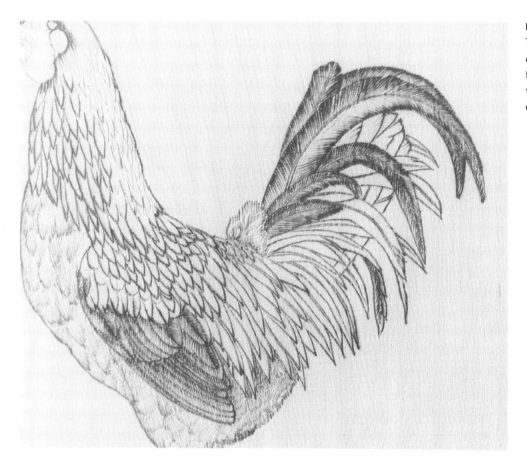

Fig 11.18
The spoon point is used to
create the texture of the main
tail feathers and the lower
wing feathers in a series of
deeply cut lines.

reason, apply a coat of permanent white in the areas shown (*see* Fig 11.19). Another advantage of using a white undercoat is that when other colours are applied and mixed into it, you will get a more solid cover than if you applied the colour directly on to the wood.

Now, with the pyrography completed except for the head and feet, you can begin to paint in the large areas of colour. I have found that it pays to be a little mean with the amount of paint to ensure that the engraved lines are not filled in. The undercoat of white will ensure that the paint covers the wood and that there is no 'show through'. Note how the painting should be begun on the head (*see* Fig 11.20). The white and red on the comb will be fused together with a slightly damp brush to form the required colour. This is a technique that works particularly well with gouache on wood.

Now turn your attention to the neck of the bird. The deep lines pyrographed to

show the feather formations are your guide to painting in the detail (*see* Fig 11.21). They will also help to steer the paint into the areas you want. It would certainly take a lot longer to produce a gouache painting of this cockerel without the help of the pyrography.

The final task to complete the illustration is to pyrograph in the beak and the feet. These two areas are well suited to a purely pyrographic treatment, and will demonstrate to any casual observer the underlying method being used here (*see* Fig 11.22).

You may want to explore this combination of painting and pyrography further. There are many other colour mediums you can use. Coloured dyes, for example, would be less likely to fill in or hide any of the pyrographic detail. Watercolours can be used for the situations that require more of a tint than a solid area of colour. Whatever method

Fig 11.19
A coat of permanent white paint is applied to the areas where lighter colours are to appear.

Fig 11.20
The application of colour.

of colouring you end up using, the pyrographic element will always serve to give the finished work that extra dimension not to be found in a conventional watercolour or similar painting.

Fig 11.21
A close-up of the neck. The deeply engraved feather outlines are a guide to the painting.

Fig 11.22
The completed cockerel, including the pyrographing of beak and feet.

CHAPTER 12

Pyrography on Woodturned Objects

There is nothing very difficult about working on non-flat surfaces. Once you have attained a reasonable pyrographic dexterity, there is no reason why you should not attempt to engrave a bowl, a rolling pin, an egg cup or any other seemingly awkward-shaped item. The most important requirement is to find a comfortable position for your hand while you work. This way, the shape of the object cannot affect the quality of your work. The project in this chapter is for solid-point machine users.

◼ How to work on curved surfaces

I have found the following to be the most effective method for working on curved surfaces; rest the heel of your hand on a raised surface adjacent to and approximately level with the surface you are about to pyrograph so that the point of the pencil is within comfortable reach of the wood, as it would be when working on a flat surface. Your other hand can hold the handle or edge of the object, rotating it slowly as you progress with your design (*see* Fig 12.1).

Working with a bowl or vase on your lap, on the other hand, is not a good idea. Similarly, placing an object on the table in front of you and trying to position your body and your hand so that you can pyrograph a vertical line is making things hard for yourself.

◼ The project

The bowl used in the following project (*see* Fig 12.2) is supplied by Janik. My design deliberately covers the more inaccessible parts of the bowl, partly to demonstrate that it is not that difficult, and partly because these are the parts that will be on display; after all, if the bowl is used for its purpose, the pot pourri would cover any design pyrographed on the bottom anyway.

Before attempting any pyrography, ensure that you have sufficient scrap sheets or pieces of ply to make a stack approximately the same height as the depth of the bowl. (I have sometimes used an old hardback book for this in the past, providing that the book has been broad enough to rest my hand on it.) I am looking for a bold and heavy design so I have used the Janik G4 machine for this piece with four attachments (nos. 22, B21, B24 and 25).

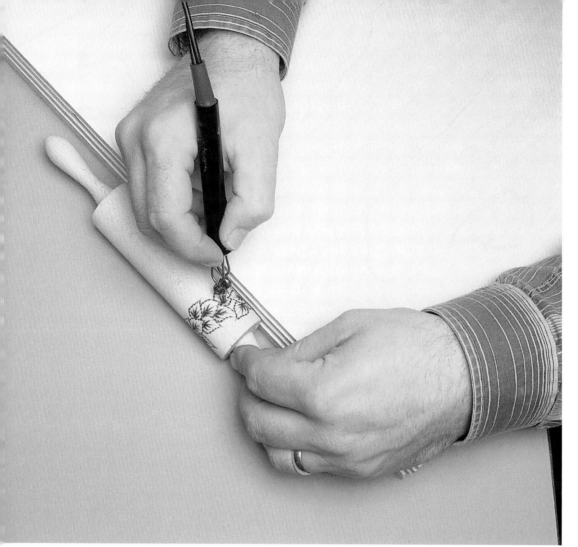

Fig 12.1
Pyrographing a design on a rolling pin. The hand is resting on a stack of ply sheets to bring it level with the surface that is being worked on.

Tracing the design

Tracing a repeat design on a curved surface can cause minor difficulties; the secret here is to use as a basis a design of a size that will sit *in* the curve rather than around it. The focal point of my design is a simple drawing of a dog rose. The original line illustration was drawn approximately 1¹/₈in (29mm) across. Use the more traditional tracing technique of covering the reverse of the drawing with soft pencil carbon.

Before going any further you will need to mark the boundaries of your design on the rim and inside the bowl. For the inside you will need a small plate, a saucer, or a round lid, that will sit inside the bowl exposing only the area to be worked on. Hold the inverted receptacle firmly in position, and mark a soft pencil line around it (*see* Fig 12.3). For the rim, build a stack of ply up to the desired level and, with the bowl butted up to the edge of the ply place a soft pencil on top of the

stack. Make sure that the pencil lead just overhangs the stack enough to touch the rim in the position you need it, and then, holding the pencil in position with one hand, carefully rotate the bowl with the other hand until you have made a pencil line all the way round it (*see* Fig 12.4). You can now trace on your flower design.

Cut out your photocopy of the flower leaving just enough white paper around so it can be stuck with masking tape to the

Fig 12.2
A sycamore pot pourri bowl 8¹/₂in (216mm) in diameter and 2in (50mm deep), supplied by Janik.

bowl; not too much though: the larger the paper the harder it is to work it round the curve. Attach it in this way at the top of the flower and the side. Then place a single piece of ply on your work surface and position the bowl on its rim against the far edge of the ply with the inside of the bowl facing you. The area to be worked on will now be an extension of the ply, providing that the thickness of the rim of the bowl is approximately equal to the thickness of the ply (*see* Fig 12.5).

I have arranged my flowers in varying positions; the calculations needed to make the design symmetrical could no doubt be made, but I prefer the more free design. In fact you will notice that my flowers have been placed in different

rotations and two of them have encroached inside the inner boundary. Be careful when working in this way that you keep an eye on the spaces between these tracings. I have deliberately spaced them very slightly unevenly, checking when I had three or four more to trace that I had a reasonable amount of room to fit the last two in, keeping a balanced design.

Pyrographing the lines

Once the flowers are all in place they can be pyrographed. I used a no. B21 point for these outlines, set at near-maximum temperature. The only concern here is that, fairly obviously, some of the lines are going to be with the grain, and others will be against it. Use some pressure and be positive, or else risk allowing the grain to dictate where the point is to travel.

Where one of the flowers appears inside the

Fig 12.3
An inverted saucer is placed inside the bowl and a pencil line is drawn around its rim to mark the inner boundary of the design.

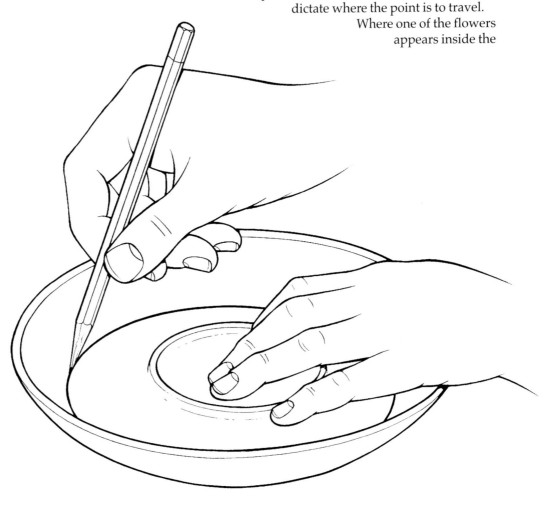

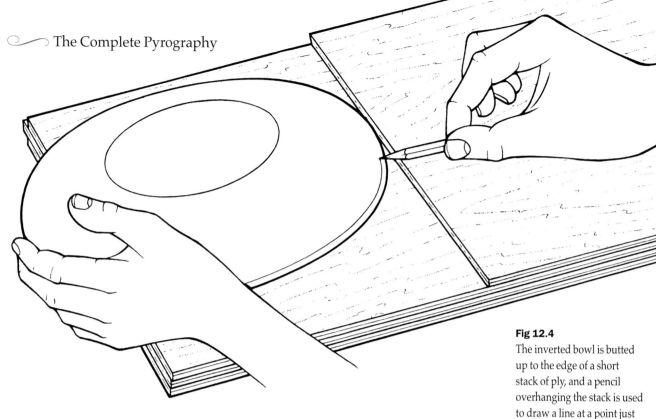

inner edge of the design it is easier to pyrograph it by reaching across it with the bowl standing normally. Where the petals have reached slightly onto the top of the rim, you need to return to making a stack of ply equal to the depth of the bowl, and then place the bowl right side up butted up to the edge of the stack (*see* Fig 12.6). The bulk of the pyrographed petals however can be produced by placing the bowl in the position described for the tracing (*see* page 100).

Pyrographing the boundaries

The rest of the pyrography involves the production of textures. I am always in favour of completing the more problematic sections early, thereby alleviating in part the risk of making a serious mistake towards the end of a piece of work. With this in mind, the suggested option is to mark in the lines at the edges of the design first. For this I have used a no. B24 point set at the maximum temperature setting. This is probably the most nerve-racking part of the whole operation. I have found the best way to position the bowl for this stage is to hold it rather like a discus, supported against your body with the work area on the edge of the table (*see* Fig 12.7). Again a

Fig 12.4
The inverted bowl is butted up to the edge of a short stack of ply, and a pencil overhanging the stack is used to draw a line at a point just below the rim. This marks the outer boundary of the design.

Fig 12.5
For tracing the design on the inner bowl, the rim of the bowl is butted up to a single sheet of ply so that the area being worked on becomes an extension of the ply.

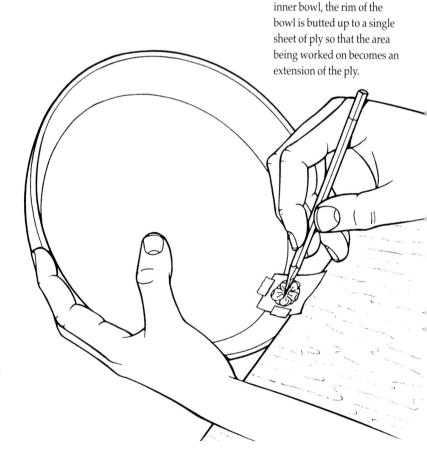

single sheet of ply will raise the level of the point to enable you to simulate working on a flat surface. Lean the bowl so it is angled slightly away from the hand with the pencil and then gradually rotate it at intervals as you carefully pyrograph a line of dots along the inner pencil line boundary. If a dot or two strays inside the line you will not incur a problem, but you must be careful not to wander over the other side of the line. You need to show a

Adding texture

The worst is now over; what remains is to add the various textures to complete this piece of work. The pencil lines having been covered, further work in the same manner should now be carried out to thicken these lines up. Working round the inside of the bowl, carefully put in the marks outside the outline of the petals, slowly increasing the texture area. This is

Fig 12.6
To pyrograph the top of the rim, butt the bowl up to the edge of a stack of ply the same height as the bowl.

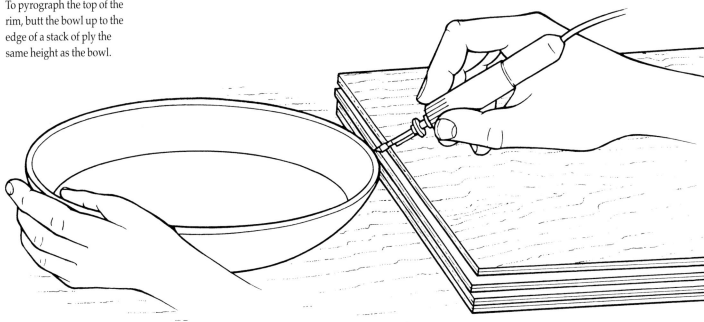

consistent and accurate set of marks.

Marking in a similar line on the outside edge of the bowl requires the construction of a simple ramp. The way I tackled this was to lean a single sheet of ply against an old hardback book. The hand holding the pyrography pencil rests on the book while the bowl is placed upside down on the ply (*see* Fig 12.8). It is important to direct the light from your angle-poise lamp on to the area you are working. This is because you will have to work at a slight angle to the surface you are engraving, and a clear view is crucial if you are to follow the pencil guide line accurately.

a laborious task, but it serves the beneficial purpose of highlighting the flowers within the rest of the design.

Using the cutting edge of a no. 25 point, the next texture can be pyrographed. This is a simple matter of producing groups of cuts, usually four at a time. Work from the dark texture around each flower and similarly from the boundary line, leaving occasional gaps for the addition of the final texture. For the final texture, revert to point no. B21, this time working with it more quickly to give a similarly dark but smaller mark. This same mark can be produced along the top of the bowl's rim.

103

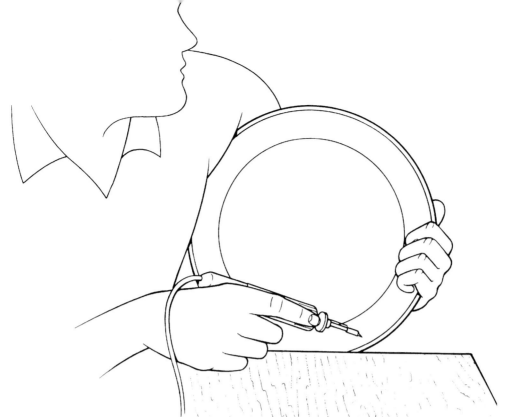

Fig 12.7
To pyrograph the dotted lines at the inner edge of the design, hold the bowl firmly in the crook of your arm with the rim against your shoulder and the area to be worked on against the edge of the table.

Fig 12.8
To burn the dotted lines at the outer edge of the design, tilt a sheet of ply against a hardback book, then place the inverted bowl on the ply and rest your pyrographing hand on the book.

Finally, to link these small, dark, round marks to the groups of cut marks, and to cover the rim top, simply repeat this process, but at a reduced temperature setting.

I looked long and hard at the bowl when I reached this stage before realizing what finishing touch was required – something was needed in the centres of the flowers. Selecting a no. 22 point, and setting it at the maximum temperature setting, the central part of the flower has been represented by a group of marks made by pushing the point vertically into the wood. The stamens have been shown by producing flick strokes with the same point and punctuating these with more vertically pyrographed marks.

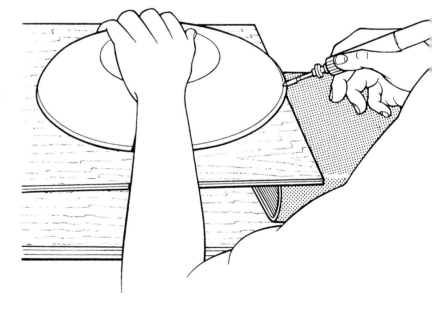

Fig 12.9
The completed pot pourri bowl.

CHAPTER 13

Advanced Pyrography

If you have progressed this far with this book, you will have picked up most of the basic skills of the craft. Now here is an opportunity to try something a bit special – a couple of quite complex illustrations which will allow you to try out all the skills you have acquired so far, and perhaps also extend your awareness of what can be achieved within this medium. Both of these projects are challenging – the cottage especially – and as well as a test of your talents, they will require all your reserves of patience. But the results, when you are finished, will hopefully be something of which you can be extremely proud.

■ Reading wagon

This project sets out to cover several aspects of pyrography at the same time. I have taken the line drawing (*see* Fig 13.1) from a Romany book. It is clearly intended to show those interested a breakdown of the way a Romany wagon is constructed, identifying all the extraneous parts. It is of course a sketch, and a lot of detail is not seen clearly, although help is provided by the information to be found around the sketch. Subjects involving any form of timber construction nearly always produce good pyrography. A sycamore rectangular plaque of 12½ x 8½in (317 x 216mm) was used for this piece, and an involved piece of work such as this would not normally be used to adorn a utensil. I would recommend the use of birch-faced ply or a veneer so that the finished work can be framed in a conventional way.

Tracing the original

Having decided on the surface you are going to apply it to, take a photocopy of the drawing to the size you require. To give you an idea of the most suitable size, I produced my photocopy to make the wagon approximately 5½in (140mm) long from the shaft ends to the steps (slung for the road). Cut out the wagon leaving enough of a border to enable you to attach the photocopy to the surface of the wood. Make sure you also have Fig 13.1 to hand (or a copy of it) to help identify the parts of the wagon.

You are now ready to trace through the copy and pencil carbon underneath (*see* Fig 13.2). Do not worry about large shadow areas at this stage; concentrate on the main lines and marks. As always, use a hard pencil (4H), and press with enough pressure to produce a fine grey visible mark. Do not jump the gun and insert any detail that you think might be there; the time to add and enhance the work will come later. Before removing the original from its position, check very carefully that nothing has been missed. If you have attached the photocopy by a single strip of masking tape, you can actually fold it away from the tracing so it can be pulled back should you discover, once you have started to burn, that some important detail has inadvertently been omitted.

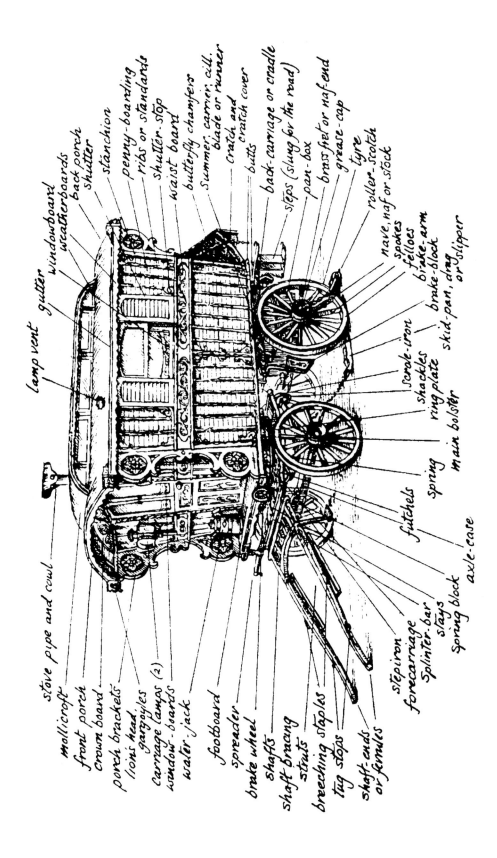

Fig 13.1
Reading wagon template.

Fig 13.2
The main lines and marks from the drawing transferred to the sycamore.

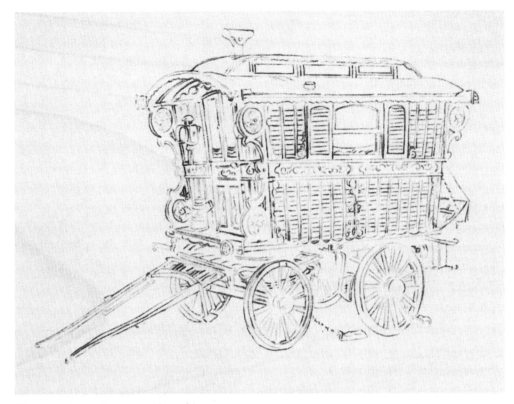

Pyrographing the lines

Before starting, set the wire point to a temperature that will allow you to apply reasonable pressure without overburning. You really want to reproduce the tracing only at this stage, making sure that you remove as much as possible of the carbon lines (*see* Fig 13.3).

Sometimes the initial problem comes with deciding where to actually make a start. It is best to choose a place that has a few simple lines together. If you have ever done any sketching you will no doubt be used to applying yourself to large areas of an illustration at a time. This kind of pyrography – like any form of engraving – restricts you to working on very small areas and lines at a time. Wherever you decide to begin, work slowly and carefully on that one area. This first stage is probably the most important one. Try burning a few trial marks on a scrap of similar material, before turning to the actual tracing. To burn too fiercely or too faintly will cause problems later. Continue until the whole

tracing has been pyrographed (*see* Fig 13.4).

Beginning the shading

Referring back to the original, take some time to study where the lines are thicker and perhaps weightier. There should be no need to adjust the temperature setting; darker lines and marks can be achieved by using a little more pressure and working a little slower. Fig 13.1 suggests that on many of the boards and brackets there is decorative carving. This has been implied by the artist without actually supplying any detail. If you burn straight lines and ignore this carving, the visual flavour of the subject will be lost. To help you, study the strut running along the bottom of the side of the wagon. This clearly shows sections that have been neatly carved out of the wood. It would be fair to assume that the ribs – or standards as they are known – running vertically over the horizontal penny boarding, would have been carved for decoration in the same way. When you

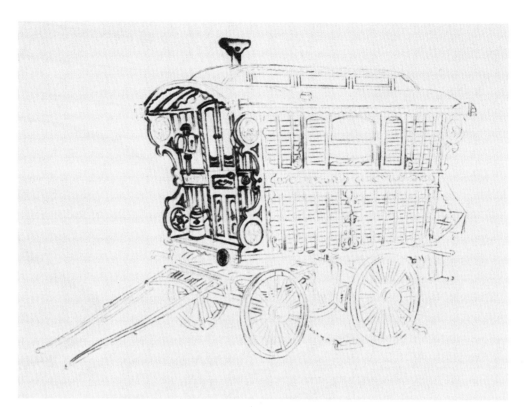

Fig 13.3
The line pyrography begun.

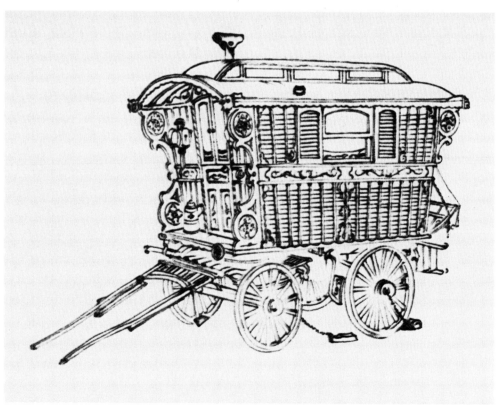

Fig 13.4
The line pyrography
completed.

were tracing, and again when burning away the trace lines, you probably just showed all these as straight lines.

It is at this stage, when you are really studying the piece and burning in the thicker lines, that the pyrograph will be begin to come to life (*see* Fig 13.5). There is no need to worry about large shadow areas at this point, but where there are smaller solid lines and areas, carefully put them in. The wheels should be treated in this way, and also some of the little areas that denote various parts of the undercarriage. A lot of what is going on under the wagon is not clear; the finished pyrograph will show most of this in shadow, so do not worry about it at this stage.

If you have already had a go at the project featuring the hinge design (*see* Chapter 10, you will understand how careful shading can give life to a piece of pyrography. Take your time with this stage; look very carefully and see where the small dark lines and areas of minute dark shading can collectively enhance the overall effect. The shutters on either side of the window are constructed from angled overlapping boards to admit air and exclude rain when closed. Intermittent shading down each side of the shutters is a simple way of showing the construction of the subject. This may sound like a statement of the obvious, but it is very common for students to interpret such areas as simple lines and then wonder afterwards why their work appears a touch flat and boring. Similarly, careful study needs to be made of the whole of the front of the wagon. There are many small areas, e.g. directly under the crown boards of the front porch, the lamp, behind the water jack and under the footboard, that all require carefully and slowly pyrographed dark lines – the darker the better.

Shading with the wire point

A spoon point can be used to produce many of the shading effects, but sometimes you will find, especially when working on the smaller areas of shading,

Fig 13.5
The thicker lines burned in.

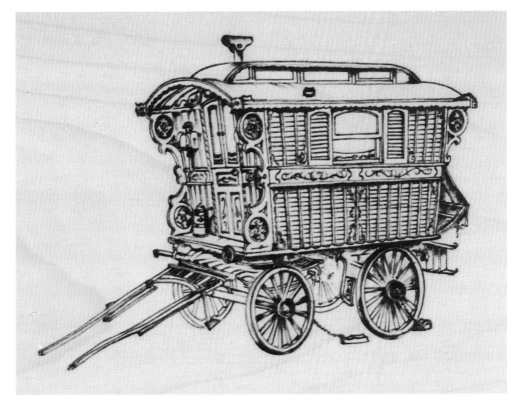

that it is better to stick with the wire point. A good example of this is the darkened area below the weatherboard directly above the side window. The dark shading here clearly shows the shape of the bottom of the weatherboard. The shading with the wire point on this part of the wagon is achieved by slowly, and with a fair amount of pressure, burning a dark line along the bottom of the weatherboard to form a groove. It is then a case of working vertically, using short strokes, from the groove downwards. The problem with using the spoon point for this comes when you reach the top of the shutters; there is just not enough room to shade comfortably with the larger tool.

The main roof and the mollicroft, whether stretched with fabric or constructed with shaped wooden boards, also have a texture that is best suggested by use of the wire point. Using a lower temperature setting, pyrograph a series of touching lines following the curves already suggested in the original drawing. Use plenty of pressure when you are doing this to obtain the textured effect (*see* Fig 13.6). Make sure before you attempt this that you have had sufficient

practice on a scrap piece of wood first; you are now well into this piece of pyrography and are at what I call the dangerous stage. It is normally at this point that the temptation arises to speed up the work. Disaster can occur in the form of a too-hot point that was not tested first – so beware!

Probably the trickiest section in this project is the delicate shading that represents the glass in the window. Again this has been done with the wire point, but at an even lower temperature setting. As you can see, it is just a series of angled lines. However, you must be very careful on this occasion not to use an excess of pressure; you are trying to denote a suggestion of reflection rather than texture.

Shading with the spoon point

If you are now satisfied that all the work with the wire point has been completed, it is time to think about the shading that can be more easily done with the spoon point. The advantage of the spoon point over the wire point is that, if used correctly, it can produce both hard, ridged lines as in the blackberry panel design (*see* pages 66 – 70), as well as the more gentle and subtle untextured shading which is the requirement here. Certainly a little practice beforehand is a must. Set the temperature low until you are able to

Fig 13.6
The roof of the wagon pyrographed to suggest the curves and texture of the original.

Fig 13.7
Further shading done on the side of the wagon, extending the shadow areas with graduated tones.

Fig 13.8
One of the darker areas beneath the wagon burned in using the spoon point.

produce small areas of approximately
¼in (6mm) square of light shading. As a
guide, you are looking for a colouring
similar to that obtained with the wire-
point shading on the roof. If you can
achieve this, then – with a little alteration
of pressure and speed, and without
having to further alter the temperature
setting – you will have at your disposal a
substantial range of dark and light. Now
you can begin to add the final touches of
shading. Start with the side of the wagon
first, gently continuing with the various
areas begun darkly with the point to give
a more extended and gradual area of tone
(*see* Fig 13.7). It is important that you
constantly refer to the original while
doing this.

The underneath of the wagon is bound
to be a fairly gloomy area with little detail
visible. This is as good a place as any to
start with the spoon point. There are two
darker patches between the tops of the
wheels and the base of the wagon. To
show these, use slow, deliberate strokes
from the base of the wagon, gradually
reducing the pressure and speed as you
progress between the wheels (*see* Fig
13.8). There are very few parts of this
pyrograph that have not received the
attention of the spoon point – too many to
mention individually. At this stage, one
tends to work on the whole piece at once
as it were, adding little touches here and
there, softening the rough edges of sharp
lines from the original shading work done
with the wire point. This is an
opportunity to insert a lot of shading
detail in to the front porch, which is in my
opinion the focal point of the work. There
are lots of little sections, particularly the
wooden panels, the inside of the porch
bracket and waistboards, which require
shading (*see* Fig 13.9).

If you have reached thus far with this
project, your knowledge of the Reading
Wagon will be better than average. These
vehicles were all made individually and
were home to a whole family. A lot of care
and skill went into their construction and
they were very expensive to commission.
While you are engaged in these final stages

of the work, try to appreciate the time and
effort that the builder himself put in. It
may help you in your own efforts.

Using the grain markings

As a final part to this project, try using the
natural grain markings of the wood to
advantage. So that the wagon does not
look as if it is floating in mid-air, some
details of a landscape have been added,
suggesting earth, stones, weeds etc. The

Fig 13.9
Detail showing the porch of
the wagon, with its various
features shaded.

important thing to notice is that certain grain lines have been followed (*see* Fig 13.10). In fact, they provide the basis for the background and the foreground. Where the grain lines appear to move away behind the wagon I have toned down the effect. This is a simple and most effective way of giving the work the beginnings of depth.

A lot of pyrography has been covered in the course of executing this project. Hopefully it has given an insight into how to convert a sketch or drawing as opposed to a life study or photograph. It has offered plenty of opportunities to produce consistent lines of varying length – something that is always difficult for beginners in pyrography – and it has also included some interesting and varied methods of shading, both with the wire point and the spoon point.

Finally, it has shown how consideration can be given to the natural markings of the wood.

◼ Cottage

If you go to enough craft venues, demonstrating your skills and displaying your best and most saleable work – regardless of whether your display includes any landscapes or property illustrations – you are bound to be asked sooner or later to consider this type of commission. There are many people interested in works of art recording their properties. Quite often the client will not be the owner of the property, but someone wishing to bestow a gift on the friend 'who has everything'.

When in the past I have been asked to

Fig 13.10

The grain lines of the sycamore are followed when pyrographing the background and foreground, thereby placing the wagon in context.

Fig 13.11
The original upon which this pyrograph is based.

do this, I have often found it to be quite a challenge pyrographically. Clearly no two houses are ever the same, and each time I have attempted to pyrograph one a whole new set of difficulties have had to be resolved. This makes it hard to set down a method for a student to follow. I have therefore decided to write a commentary on this particular project as I progress through it. As the piece unfolds I will explain my own attempts to create the effects I need. I am not suggesting right or wrong ways of doing things; if you have followed the book this far you will certainly have your own ideas about such a quest. What I can say is that nothing gives me more pleasure than to overcome all the obstacles and achieve a result.

Photographing the property

Although in the past I have, for practical reasons, worked entirely from a photograph, there can never be a better way of starting such a project than to visit the scene personally and take your own photographs. If you are able to do this, study the scene carefully and take a selection of at least three shots from slightly varying angles. Even though you will probably have decided very quickly on the view you want, still take those extra shots. I have in the past taken a single view of the building only to find, once I have begun, that a chimney or part of the roof is obscured by foliage. However good you think your memory might be, or even if you suspect the roof and chimneys are identical at either end of the house, a couple of photographs showing these aspects would have alleviated any doubts on this score. Once a decision on which photograph to use has been made, photocopy it. In this case, the size I am working to is 150% of the photograph in Fig 13.11.

Selecting the wood and the position

The next thing to do is to select the piece

of wood, and then the part of it I am going to work on. Because of the numbers of bricks and tiles etc., there are going to be many more lines travelling horizontally than vertically in this piece, and you will help yourself by selecting a wood surface in which the grain travels in a horizontal direction. Looking through my current collection of pieces of birch-faced plywood I find that the grain is moving in the wrong direction in all of them! These things happen, and on this occasion I have to settle for a piece of birch-faced ply, where the vertical grain lines have spread out towards what will be the top of the picture. A lot of engraving is concentrated in small areas, so I am not anticipating a major problem with the grain showing through. Remember, when attempting to burn a consistent and continuous line against the grain, a little less speed and a little more patience is required.

I position the building slightly to the left of centre of a piece of wood 12 x 18in (305 x 457mm). I do not expect there to be a problem when the piece is framed; this off-centredness can be compensated for by careful positioning of the overlay mount, with extra plywood packed into the frame behind the mount if necessary. With everything now in position, I am able to start transferring my working plan onto the wood surface.

Tracing the plan

I am not going to trace all of the picture with every last brick and tile faithfully represented. My method of tracing should enable me to mark the wood very lightly in the areas where I need to show detail; further drawing can then be done by hand directly on to the wood to complete the picture plan.

I normally select one of the outlines of the building as my starting point, and in this case I choose the row of tiles at the apex of the roof. As I have already said, each tile and brick will not be recorded with photographic precision, but rather an accurate impression of them needs to be

created. This is not the case with the outline of the roof which, if produced with the undulations in the wrong places or with the tiles themselves inaccurately shaped and sized, will offend the eye and be immediately noticeable. I therefore take as much care as possible to recreate them. When I am satisfied that I have achieved the necessary density and clarity of this first traced section, I can continue with the plan. I use a very sharp 6H pencil, sharpened with a scalpel blade, and every so often I resharpen the point.

Once the most prominent lines have been dealt with, that is to say the outline of the chimney, guttering, window frames etc., I turn my attention to marking out where the trees, shrubs and foliage are going to be. A small, leafy tree in the foreground partially obscures the right-hand side of the property. Showing this will be difficult: the roof tiles and odd bits of brickwork behind the tree must really be engraved before the leaves and foliage; it is extremely difficult to do it the other way round. This is where the photocopy and its loss of detail will actually assist you. Starting with the leaves and branches that have only sky as background, I trace through the photocopy some of the individual leaves, adding others that may or may not actually be there, but keeping a careful watch that the overall impression is one of quantity and density. Remember to have at hand your actual photograph to remind you of what the photocopy has been unable to reproduce. I then work my way down the whole of the right-hand side of the picture tracing all the gaps between the leaves and branches. This will allow you to draw and trace enough of the partially obscured bricks, leaving the areas where foliage can be engraved, clear.

As far as the rest of the many trees and shrubs are concerned, I simply mark in the outlines of them, including lines to show where one shrub meets the outline of another. There is a rather nice and well-established wisteria supported by a metal frame and spreading from its roots behind a low thick shrub to the front porch in one direction, and to an end window in the other. This is the sort of feature that is important if you are going to properly recreate this view and I make sure it is marked in accurately, including the position of the branches as they twist up the wall.

There is very little showing of the actual front door, even on the photograph, and I make no attempt to presume what I cannot see. The heavily shaded area within the porch is a focal point of the picture and, when the time comes, it will need to be made as dark as possible.

The next task is to decide how best to show the tiles and bricks. As a texture the roof is very interesting and can only be reproduced by a multitude of varying marks. The photocopy has actually highlighted these, but it would not be practicable to trace the whole thing, particularly at the size dictated by the scale of the work. I therefore trace odd areas of the roof as accurately as I can, marking in the horizontal lines first. I then fold the photocopy back and, using the original photograph as a guide, draw in the remaining horizontal lines. Where the tiles go behind the foliage, I run the lines slightly into the leaves, knowing that the unwanted pencil marks can easily be burned away. At this stage I am not worrying about the tiny vertical marks that will individualize each tile.

The brickwork has been treated more carefully with regard to detail, although I do not intend to record each brick as it actually appears in reality. The roof tiles vary slightly in size and appear to be misshapen; therefore the roof is composed of a series of slightly undulating lines. This is not the case with the brickwork, however, which is set in blocks defined by the timbers. To ensure accuracy, I have used a ruler, and traced enough of the bricks to allow me to pencil in the positions of the remainder. This use of a ruler will no doubt make the accomplished sketcher or watercolourist raise an eyebrow or two. I make no

apology, having decided that I must clearly show the contrast between bricks and tiles. To reproduce the effects I need with a heated point of wire I will have to turn the wood in a direction that allows me to pull the point towards me. When you are working in this way, you cannot view the work in the way that these other art forms allow, so the accuracy of your working plan is essential.

The use of a ruler is also desirable for defining the window frames. The frames in which the panes of glass are fitted are very narrow, and the panes themselves will be shown as darker areas with the framework in relief, but it is still important to mark their positions. The windows partly concealed by shrubbery, as with the above-mentioned brickwork, can be marked in pencil running into the foliage.

Finally, I mark the lines that determine the position of the lawn, drive and a paved path leading from the front door through the lawn. I am reasonably sure that I have all the detail I need to begin the pyrography, but I leave the photocopy taped on the wood, folded out of the way. Should I discover that some important detail was missed, or incorrectly marked on the wood, I can refer back to the photocopy. In the case of this piece of work, there are some details to be traced at a later stage, so it must remain anyway. I am now ready to make a start on the actual pyrography.

Starting on the roof tiles

The first burn line or mark is a nervous one. Given that the tracing and drawing of the plan has probably taken over two hours so far, the risk of producing the wrong kind of mark at the start must be minimized. Therefore I place a scrap of similar plywood next to the wood I am working on. The first pyrographed lines are going to be the side of the visible chimney stack, and the outline of the top of the roof. Before attempting these lines, one with the grain and one against, I have had a couple of trial runs on the scrap surface. Only when I am sure that the temperature setting and the amount of pressure used to make the mark are right, will I attempt to make a start.

The roof tiles on this building are magnificent, and to create them properly will take a lot of time. Turning the surface through 90 degrees, I make a start with the horizontal lines. This is fairly simple to do and gives me an initial feel for the task ahead. After producing several lines, I turn my attention to the round tiles at the top of the roof. Working a little more slowly and deliberately the outlines are completed, and then I return to finish the horizontals of the tiles (see Fig 13.12).

Windows

At this stage I decide to start working on the windows. I admit to being nervous at continuing with the roof tiles, and like to see some more heavily burned areas early on. Furthermore, it is wise to start considering the balance of light and dark as soon as possible.

With the exception of the panes of glass that reflect natural sky light because they are angled towards it, most of the glass will be shown as small dark areas (see Fig 13.13). For this reason I presume that the tool to use is the spoon point, and I use it for the first window (top left). I soon realize I am wrong. The areas are simply too small; to have a chance of raising the narrow frames from the glass you need to apply pressure, and the only way to do this is to use the wire point very slowly, at a low temperature setting, and using a lot of pressure. There is no need to burn the framework around the glass; it is more effective to represent the glass panes alone and leave the rest in relief.

Do not forget, while you work on the windows, to slightly overlap the lines that will contain the various areas of foliage. It should not appear as if the windows etc. stop abruptly where they meet the bushes, but rather that they continue on behind. I now start to pyrograph some of the leaf outlines that will obscure parts of the windows on the right-hand side of the picture. One of the difficulties that I am going to face with this piece is the obscuring of the subject with leaves and various clumps of foreground foliage.

Adding these darker window areas has brought some life to the work in the same way that adding the mouse's eye early in that project did (see Chapter 9). There may be additional work required on the windows, but until I have begun work on the various areas of foliage I will not proceed further.

Spoon point work

The very heavily shaded area within the porch is a focal point of the work as I suspected it would be. It is always more difficult to achieve that extra-dark effect on birch ply; sycamore is really the best material for this effect. I use the spoon point at the lowest temperature setting that will make a mark, and work very slowly indeed, pressing as hard as I can without bending the point, to produce this dark area. Similarly, while the spoon point is handy, I add further dark lines representing the shadow formed by the roof guttering and the lower row of tiles near it. A similar shaded area exists on the roof of the porch. All of these areas and lines have been carried out slowly and carefully with the spoon point. Where a narrower mark has been needed, the edge of the spoon has been used.

Brickwork and more on roof tiles

Another fundamental part of this project is going to be the portrayal of the brickwork. There are clearly two distinct sections here: the brickwork of the house and the brickwork of the chimney stack. The latter appears to be made from smaller bricks, which is probably an illusion brought about by the chimney being further away, and the fact that the chimney bricks are darker.

The scale of my picture dictates that rather than attempt to reproduce every brick faithfully and individually, I am looking to provide merely an impression of what is going on. The way I approach this is to trace through the photocopy some sample areas of the chimney and the brickwork at the front of the building, and then, within the outlines of bushes etc., draw in the remaining brickwork as a texture with a soft pencil, using my traced sections as a guide to position and size.

Once you have got everything down lightly in pencil, you need to take a deep breath and make a start. If you are starting with the chimney as I am, you really want to try and finish it in one session. Coming back to finish the other half a day later is never a good idea.

I have to say at this stage that I am not too excited at my own result so far. In retrospect I think I could have made things a lot easier for myself if I had worked from a larger size. However, there is a lesson to be learnt even from this situation. There will be times when, some hours into a project, niggling doubts may occur; you may not be entirely happy with the way a piece of work is going, and you may not even know why straight away. My advice is to stop work immediately and leave it alone for a day or two, if you can. When you return you will often immediately see what is wrong and how it can be remedied. I have frequently felt like abandoning a piece of work, but I have very rarely actually done so.

The problem in this case is that there are three textures or areas that have to be shown in different ways to give the contrast needed, and unfortunately they are all very similar: I am talking about the roof tiles and the two types of brickwork. My method of showing two different brick textures is to produce them in two different ways.

The chimney bricks comprise solid marks made with the flat of the wire point. In other words, each brick is represented by a single mark. I have turned the surface through 90 degrees so that the marks can be made by pulling the point towards me. Extra care must be taken if you are, like me, working against

Fig 13.12
The rooftop and one side of the chimney stack have been outlined, and the roof tiles begun.

Fig 13.13
The window panes have
been burned in.

the grain of the wood. Before starting on the bricks, it helps to apply enough pressure to the point to sufficiently bend it against a piece of scrap wood, giving the point a shape that will allow the maximum point surface area to make contact with the surface of the wood. Each mark can be varied by altering pressure and speed to show the differences in light and dark of the bricks (*see* Fig 13.14).

At this juncture there can be no more cowardice in the face of the roof tiles; a start on the roof must be attempted. I think my fear stems from the fact that I have the original photograph in front of me clearly showing the intricacies of the colour and texture within the roof. It is important to keep an eye on perspective and, as shown in Fig 13.14, I rule in a series of vertical lines to make sure the correct angles of the tiles are shown. Bearing in mind that I have some actual

traced areas of tiles as a guide, it is a simple though monotonous task to pencil in the rest of them (or at least a representative area). The horizontal lines have already been pyrographed in of course, and the next task is to work through the rows, carefully and more or less individually outlining each tile. You will be able to work fairly quickly; do not use too much heat, and apply a reasonable pressure, enough to make a positive indentation into the surface. The tiles also have a slight curve to their shape. I have attempted to show this by the addition of some short curved lines at the bottom edge of the tiles, using the cutting edge of the spoon point.

When working on a piece such as this, I tend to flit from section to section. Because I have elected to write about this as I am actually doing it I have had to be a little more ordered in my methods. However, please do not feel that each section must be completed before moving on to the next. If you suddenly feel that it would help you to work on some of the foliage, then do so. Of if you feel that the tiles or bricks are just not working as you would wish and you need a break, then take one. My only advice is to make sure that you can easily return to a section and continue it in the same style as you left it.

The bricks at the front of the house

Starting the foliage

Before any despondency is allowed to creep in I turn my attention temporarily to the bushes and shrubs in the beds at the front of the house. The best way to start this is to spend a little time marking in with a pencil as many of the dark shaded areas as possible. The trees, shrubs, flowers and lawn represent no small task. I am going to spend a little time working

Fig 13.14
The porch area has been shaded, the brickwork on the walls and the chimney have been pyrographed, and further work done on the roof tiles.

have been pencilled in and all I do now is lightly go over the pencil marks with the wire point, and then gently shade them in.

I have now treated the roof tiles and the two areas of brickwork in the ways described, but they are all still looking too similar in terms of density. While I decide how to deal with this, I darken the roof area by shading it with the spoon point, working horizontally from the top down to the guttering. I also select various tiles and darken them to correspond with the darker tiles in the photograph.

on these while at the same time working out in my mind how to deal with the problem of the bricks and tiles.

The answer is not to be frightened by the task; armed with a pencil, look closely for the small, dark areas that mark the outlines of the various bushes, where one shrub appears in front of another. If you keep working away, sketching in and recording what you see, you will build up a very accurate plan from which to work, and at the same time you will learn more about the way the picture is to be handled. You will need to spend a fair amount of time experimenting and trying out different marks on a piece of scrap material. Try not to be nervous about using high temperatures with these test pieces. If you have one of the samplers to hand (*see* Chapter 6), look at the squares that were created with increased temperatures for inspiration. With the foliage, all you are trying to do is produce a series of light and dark areas of texture (*see* Fig 13.15).

Wood dye

Still unhappy about my failure to satisfactorily differentiate between the three areas of brickwork and roof tiles, I decide to incorporate the use of some wood dye. Wood dye or stain must be applied with extreme care. The dye has a tendency to spread, and the slightest excess may cause it to invade areas other than those to be stained.

There are various manufacturers of wood dye, and they all seem to provide a similar product. For this job I am using Blackfriar penetrating stain produced by E. Parsons and Sons of Bristol, for the simple reason that they supply a colour called Spanish Mahogany, which is very close to the colour I need.

Using a small sable brush – certainly nothing larger than a No. 1 – load it from the tin and apply to the scrap wood. This will show you how the initial coat colours the wood, and also demonstrates how careful you will need to be. Although close to the right colour it is a little weak and thin. You can either apply more coats or, as I do, pour a little of the dye into a small receptacle (like the lid of the tin), and wait for some of it to evaporate. The longer it is left, the darker the colour becomes. Make sure that almost all of the dye has been wiped off the brush before you apply it to the surface of the wood. There will still be enough on the brush to do the job, but you will be in control of the flow. Using a smaller brush (No. 00), I colour in a few of the bricks at the front of the house with the same dye. Now I feel I am nearer to achieving the result I am

looking for (*see* Fig 13.16).

Another problem now arises with the expanse of the roof tiles directly behind the tree in the right foreground. When applied to the bare wood surface, the dye is a very different colour to that applied to the pyrographed roof. I am going to be doing some very heavy burning to show the leaves in the foreground and I want a better background colour. The problem is solved by burnishing or burning lightly the bare surface with the convex side of a spoon point, and then adding the dye.

Foliage continued

I am now pleased enough with the work on the building to concentrate properly on finishing the bushes, shrubs and trees – in particular the tree in the foreground. I have always known how I was going to tackle the larger leaves: plenty of heat and a red-hot spoon point. Practise on a piece of scrap, using the cutting edge of the spoon point as a gouge. The red-hot point will carve into the wood very quickly, so be careful. The odd visible twigs and branches can be created with the edge of the point, and the denser areas with the more commonly used convex side of the spoon point. Keep an eye out for the darker areas; you are aiming to show the tree with the cottage just visible through it. I am pleased with my efforts here, especially with the contrast against the roof tiles (*see* Fig 13.17).

It should be fairly easy to see how the various other leaves and branches have been formed. The answers can be found in the samplers if you are in doubt (*see* Chapter 6). The exception might be the bush that appears to be sprouting from the area halfway down the chimney stack. This was done in the same way as described for the large tree on the right-hand side, but with a much reduced temperature setting.

The final problem is deciding at which point to stop work. It is important not to overwork the piece and risk spoiling it. You could opt for a little more colour.

Fig 13.15
The roof tiles completed,
work is begun on the foliage.

Some carefully added tints to the foliage would certainly show off the brickwork. I have decided that, apart from the added dye, my piece will remain purely pyrographic. I have made a rough paper overlay mount to show what will be visible when the piece is finally framed. It is a good idea to do that at this stage to help determine how far out to the edges you can work to.

I hope you will have got something of value from this exercise. It was quite a long and complex project, involving many different pyrographic techniques, and do not be put off if you do not achieve quite what you hoped for. It shows just what is possible within the medium of pyrography and will hopefully encourage people to go beyond the simple and the commonplace and attempt something a little more ambitious.

Fig 13.16
The roof tiles coloured with wood dye.

Fig 13.17
The completed cottage.

CHAPTER 14

Protecting the Finished Pyrograph

Unless a work is to be framed behind glass like a picture, then some protection such as a varnish or a polish will be necessary. Pyrographs that are likely to be handled frequently – boxes, for example – are especially vulnerable to wear. Another hazard is direct sunlight.

◼ The effects of direct sunlight on unprotected wood

Some years ago I left a few of my craft items with friends to display in their village shop. The shop closed recently and the pieces were returned to me. They had been displayed in the shop window as part of a display of local crafts, and the shop proprietor had attached labels to them. The slight colour change that they had undergone was not noticed until I removed the labels. A gentle sanding with fine, used sandpaper restored them to their former glory (plus a little repyrographing of some of the detail), but I learned that one had to be a little more selective when choosing places to display unprotected work.

It is important to be aware of the effects of direct sunlight. Over a prolonged period it has a tendency to marginally darken most wood surfaces, and the ultraviolet rays contained within sunlight will, over time, reduce the density of finely burned lines or marks.

◼ Types of finish

For a good gloss finish, any sort of polyurethane varnish is recommended; yacht varnish, bearing in mind the purpose for which it was specifically designed, is particularly hard wearing. Apply as many coats as your patience will allow; the more coats, the deeper the shine.

For a polished finish, apply two coats of any acrylic varnish (preferably clear satin). Acrylic varnish has the advantage of being very quick drying and water soluble, so your brushes can be washed in water. When completely dry, smooth very gently with very fine wire wool and solid furniture polish. After your second application of furniture polish, simply polish with a soft cloth. In the case of a box that you are planning to line with sticky-backed felt, make sure you do not get any polish on the areas where the felt is to go, or it will not stick.

◼ Handy hints

- ◼ Ensure that the wood surface you are about to apply finish to is perfectly smooth. Varnish will accentuate any scratches or blemishes on the surface.
- ◼ When using varnish or polish, the best method is always to apply several thin coats.
- ◼ When buying wire wool, always try to obtain the finest grade possible.
- ◼ Brushes are very important; I have had the best results by using make-up brushes because they do not leave brush-stroke marks.
- ◼ In an emergency (i.e. the wedding gift that must be delivered on the day), you can use several thin coats of car lacquer, available from any car accessory shop in an aerosol. However, the result is not as good, because it lacks the control of the brush method.

Fig 14.1
The key-ring on the left was finished with a polyurethane varnish.

CHAPTER 15

Gallery of Pyrography

In this chapter we take a look at the work of professional pyrographers currently practising in the UK. They all use essentially the same tools to create very different results, demonstrating the sheer range of what can be achieved within the medium of pyrography.

Richard Withers

Richard Withers was born in Tredegar, South Wales, and settled in Corris (near Machynlleth, Powys) in 1984 after many years living and working in Sweden. He took up pyrography on his return to Wales, and although most people now know him as a pyrographer, his training is in fine arts, and much of his technique stems from his background as a professional artist. All his pictures are burned freehand into the wood, and are inspired by what he sees in the grain. For this reason he calls them 'grain pictures'.

Richard's policy is to use only locally grown hardwoods, from trees felled in the interest of woodland conservation. He uses a Peter Child pyrography pen, and sells 90% of his output from where he works at the Corris Craft Centre, and through commissions. In addition to his 'grain pictures', he offers a portrait service – 'a genuine work of art on a piece of wood', as well as clocks, boxes, games, bowls, vases and a whole range of smaller items.

Fig 15.1
The Good Shepherd (elm).

Fig 15.2
Waterbaby (sycamore).

Fig 15.3
Faith (sycamore).

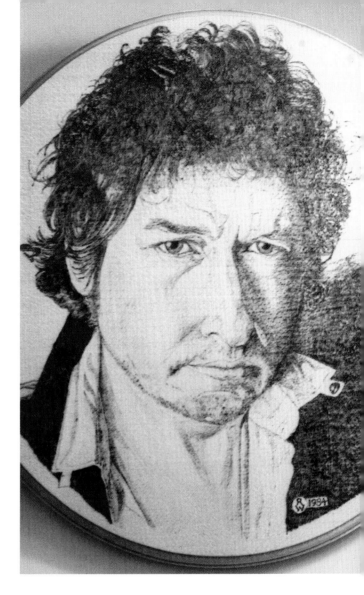

Fig 15.4
Dylan (sycamore).

Fig 15.5
A presentation clock
(sycamore) owned by
Tynycornel Hotel, Talyllyn.

127

Linda Fellows

Linda Fellows teaches classes in pyrography at the Green Lodge Adult Education Centre in Clacton-on-Sea and at Grey Friars Adult Education College in Colchester. She qualified as a teacher in 1978 and since then has taught painting and drawing as well as pyrography to both children and adults.

Linda first discovered pyrography through Stephen Poole, and has gone on to explore a range of possibilities within the craft, including experiments with paint and wood stain, pyrography on veneers, turned wood, fabric, cork, leather, and even paper. Her latest work involves a three-dimensional picture made up from layered balsa wood with the top layer pyrographed. She sells her work locally at craft fairs and exhibitions.

Fig 15.7
Colchester Siege House (sycamore).

Fig 15.6
A Country Lane (sycamore). This shows a variety of textures and offers an aeriel perspective, giving the effect of distance.

Fig 15.8
Burning Wood (sycamore).
A literal and symbolic title,
reflecting on the destruction
by burning of forests.

Fig 15.9
Zebras (sycamore). Stripes
using decreasing heat to
illustrate distance.

Terry Leverett

(of Form Crafts)

For Terry Leverett, pyrography began as a hobby in 1985, before becoming his full-time occupation four years later. He is self-taught and used his experience as an engineering draughtsman to develop a technique similar to that used by pen-and-ink artists. He uses both a Peter Child and a Janik machine, as well as one he built himself.

Terry works from a studio at his home in Derby, and exhibits throughout the year at large craft shows around the country, as well as the occasional one-man exhibition.

Of the items featured here, he finds that the hedgehog and spitfire designs are among the most popular with his customers. The Celtic design on the oblong box takes him two days to complete, and the stool takes three days.

Fig 15.10 (above)
Stephenson's Rocket
(sycamore).
© Form Crafts

Fig 15.11 (above)
An original design
(sycamore).
© Form Crafts

Fig 15.12 (right)
The North Leverton
Windmill in
Nottinghamshire (birch-
faced ply under non-
reflective glass).
© Form Crafts

Fig 15.13
This decoration on a lime wood box is based on an ancient Celtic design.
© Form Crafts

Fig 15.14
This pattern, pyrographed on a beech wood stool, was devised by Terry and based on a Celtic design.
© Form Crafts

Fig 15.15
A Mark IX Spitfire of 611 Squadron (lime).
© Form Crafts

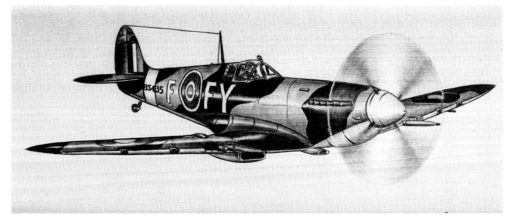

■ Siw Wood

Siw Wood's introduction to the craft came in 1990 when she inherited a 1930s vintage Bakelite pyrography machine from an aunt. She initially sold her work through craft fairs and a cooperative craftworker's shop, and in 1993, at Gatcombe Fair, she received her first Royal Commission – lettering on a platter for HRH the Princess Anne. In 1994 she opened her studio in Abersoch in Wales, which she called Oriel Coed (Gallery Wood). Since then, her work has been exhibited in art galleries, craft centres and libraries throughout North Wales.

Apart from tree pictures and dragons, Siw particularly enjoys creating large-scale illustrations of Welsh legends. The legend of the girl in the tree, featured here, has proved especially popular, prompting her to produce several smaller versions to sell. Siw welcomes commissions, specializing in commemorative plates, platters and stools.

As well as her ancient machine, Siw uses both Peter Child and Janik equipment. The wood is carefully selected so that each picture can develop naturally from its grain and texture. She paints her pyrographs with watercolours before varnishing them, and then wipes the varnish off to seal the picture with a matt finish. Then she picks out with four or more coats of varnish the parts of the picture that she wants to highlight.

Fig 15.16
A view of the display at Oriel Coed.

Fig 15.17
This was the first stool that Siw ever pyrographed – a gift for her daughter. Since then she has had about 30 commissions.

132

Fig 15.18 (right)
The top half of the legend of Rhys and Meinir, showing Meinir trapped in the tree and Rhys searching for her in vain.

Fig 15.19 (far right)
The bottom half of the legend of Rhys and Meinir, again utilizing the grain and the colour of the wood.

Fig 15.20
Commission specification: plate to include a Welsh dragon, Wales, whales, Merlin, and the schooner, *Yankee Clipper,* for which Siw was provided with a photo.

Fig 15.21
The top half of the legend of Blodeuwedd. She is being created by magic from the flowers of the oak – broom and meadowsweet. The wood grain is utilized in the shape of the hood, the direction of her arms and the 'magic' upward lines.

15.22
The bottom half of Blodeuwedd, where she is punished for plotting with her lover to kill her husband, and is turned into an owl.

CHAPTER 16

Marketing and Selling Your Work

Once you have completed a range of pyrographed items, the next stage is to try to sell them. Craft fairs are the obvious places, but other possible outlets for your work are also considered in this chapter. Also discussed here are suggestions for effective ways of displaying your work, what your display should consist of, how to communicate with the public, and how to price your work.

■ Craft fairs

Before I began teaching, I spent many years selling my pyrographic efforts at craft fairs and craft centres. Most of the time I avoided the larger functions; I found that the cost of renting stall space very rarely bore a direct relationship to the amount of advertising, and consequently the number of visitors that could be expected to attend. Where I always did best was at the smaller, local venues. The cost of renting a stall at a village or local event can be as little as £10 ($15) – a tenth of the cost of the same stall at a large weekend event, and then there are the extra travel costs to take into account. Looking at it another way, if your stall has cost £100 ($150) to rent, how many items would you need to sell after material costs and travelling expenses in order to cover the amount? So it is best to restrict yourself to the more provincial events, at least to begin with.

If you want to test the local craft scene, and, more importantly, whether the discerning public are likely to buy your wares, the best plan is to scan the local papers for advance advertisements. Village fetes and the like are nearly always advertised in this way. Even when an event is advertised only a few days in advance, there will normally be the telephone number of an organizer included. Many of these minor events suffer last-minute cancellations by stallholders, or they may simply have capacity for more vendors, in which case you can book yourself a space.

■ Your display

Now comes the most important consideration (and the one most widely

Fig 16.1
The component parts of a basic display stand, plus a few essential extras: pegboard, paste-up table, cork noticeboard, a length of 2 x 1in (50 x 25mm), nuts and bolts and spotlights.

ignored, in my opinion), which is how you display your work. To do this you will need a display table. Most village hall craft functions will be able to supply tables to the vendors, but it is very difficult to make a display of your work – however competent that work is – look attractive on a flat table. The answer is to make yourself a display stand.

Making a display stand

The paste-up table is undoubtedly the most widely used piece of equipment at craft fairs; it is no coincidence, in fact, that craft stall spaces are let in units of 6ft (1.83m) and multiples thereafter. These tables can be purchased very reasonably at any major DIY store, and I am quite sure that of the vast numbers of them sold over the last ten or so years, only a small percentage actually see use as paste-up tables.

To make a simple display stand from one of these tables it will be necessary to buy a few additional items:

- some pegboard
- some lengths of 2 x 1in (50 x 25mm)
- nuts and bolts (wing nuts are ideal)

Cut the pegboard to the length of the paste-up table, and to the height that you require (the DIY shop should do this for you). Make a supporting framework on the reverse of the pegboard around the outer edge and across the centre, with 2 x 1in (50 x 25mm). Attach another length of 2 x 1in (50 x 25mm) with wing nuts to form a support from the top of the backboard to the floor. This is important: it will help to stop the paste-up table sagging in the middle with the weight of the display. Drill and attach the backboard / supporting leg to the back of the table top. Use wing nuts for speedy assembling and dismantling.

This is a very basic display stand (*see* Fig 16.2), but it is cheap to make and certainly simple to put together. It can easily be packed into the average car while still leaving plenty of space for your boxes of craftwork.

Improving the stand

There are of course a variety of ways to improve your display stand; painting the backboard a complementary colour to your work is an obvious one. You may want to add two or more pegboard sections to the sides of the backboard, particularly if you intend to feature a lot of items that are best displayed hanging, such as keyholders, small engraved plaques and so on. Another cheap and effective display area can be created by using cork noticeboards. These can also be purchased from DIY stores, usually in various colours. Two of these, one at either end of the backboard, can be used to display key-fobs etc. They can be hung from dressmakers' pins or push pins pushed into the cork. It is always nice to see a backboard display that includes lots of small and varied items.

There is a lot more that can be done to improve the look of the stand, and thereby improve your selling chances. A sheet or cloth can be draped over the table top. Again, try and find a colour to complement the work – dark green, dark brown or blue can be attractive (*see* Fig 16.3). Make sure the cover hangs from the front of the table down to the floor. This will enable you to store things under the table without them being visible from the front of the display.

Fig 16.2
The display stand assembled.

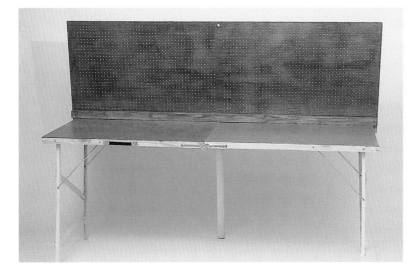

Lighting

Lighting is an absolute must. When you are applying for space at a craft function, be sure you are within reach of a power supply. It is worth having at least one extension cable in case you are not directly in front of a mains socket, ideally one with a multiple socket end. The most effective sort of lighting for your purposes is spotlighting, and the best type of spotlight is one with a clip attachment that can be positioned one at each end of the table to shine across your work (see Fig 16.3). Avoid using table lamps or work lamps for lighting your display. They are easy to knock over, and could be dangerous. If you are planning on doing any demonstrating, you will need a lamp to work under, and a work lamp is normally suitable for this purpose. Incidentally, although you may have rented a standard six foot space, if you wish to demonstrate your craft to the public – and even better if you are happy to allow people to try out your equipment for themselves – most craft fair organizers will allocate some extra space (hopefully free of charge). So be prepared and bring a small extra collapsible table for this purpose.

Props

You can do a lot to enhance your display by using 'props'. Create different levels on the table top by covering small boxes in a similar fabric and using them to display the odd item on. Flat objects such as chopping boards and breadboards look better if they are propped up in some way. You want your display to be noticed from a distance, and not just when people are practically falling over it. Light pulls, napkin rings and similar smaller items can be displayed in little wicker baskets, themselves very attractive. Collecting thimbles has always been a popular hobby, and most craft centres will have somebody selling thimble stands – an excellent way to display your thimbles. If your stock includes such items as decorated wooden bud vases, have a few dried flowers displayed in them. There are many such improvements that can be made to a display. The only real rule is to make it as interesting as you can. So often I have come across skilled crafts that have

Fig 16.3
Detail of a typical display. The cork noticeboard, which is clipped to the backboard, is used to hang the smaller items, while larger items are hung from the pegboard by wire hooks made from old coat hangers. A sheet is draped over the paste-up table.

Fig 16.4 (right)

Part of a pyrography display with items priced using both tie-on labels and the less practical method of folded price cards.

been unnoticed and therefore unsold just for the lack of a little thought and imagination in the presentation.

Displaying prices and other information

Make sure all items on your display are clearly priced. Avoid using sticky labels for pricing, as they will leave a gum deposit or stain on the wood. You may be asked to remove a label from a purchased object because it is being bought as a gift for someone. Little folded price cards next to each item can look professional until they fall over or get moved by a customer to the wrong item, causing not a little embarrassment. The best policy is to use sensibly sized tie-on labels that can show the price and maybe some additional information about the wood used or a suggested inscription (*see* Fig 16.4). If an item is sold that can be replaced by a similar one, the label can be re-used.

Customers that have made a purchase, may want to contact you in the future for more of your work, or it may be that a visiting craft fair or function organizer is impressed with your stall and would like to invite you to rent space at another event. It is therefore worth ensuring that the requisite information about yourself is available. There are several ways of doing this:

1 By attaching labels on the reverse of each item. These need not be expensive to have printed; there are many companies that offer this service. Any that you do not use can be attached to offcuts of card to make business cards which can also be left as part of your display. If you decide to do this, make sure you include information other than just your name, address and telephone number that will mark you out from the rest of the crowd. For example, if you are prepared to demonstrate at craft shows and village fairs, or if you work solely in English seasoned woods, then these are the sorts of things to mention on your card (*see* Fig

16.5). The labels can also be used to make letterheads, compliment slips and invoices.

2 If you are offering services connected with your craft such as 'commissions accepted' or 'party plan', make a small sign (pyrographed on wood if you like) to advertise this, or even better, produce some leaflets that people can take away with them.

3 A slightly more offbeat but interesting way to draw the public's attention to you and your work, is to write a few paragraphs explaining what exactly pyrography is. Have them photocopied or printed and, again, make sure details of how to find you are included in the copy. It has happened to me time and time again over the years: someone has admired my work, and then some considerable while later, being stuck for a special gift, has contacted me. This was

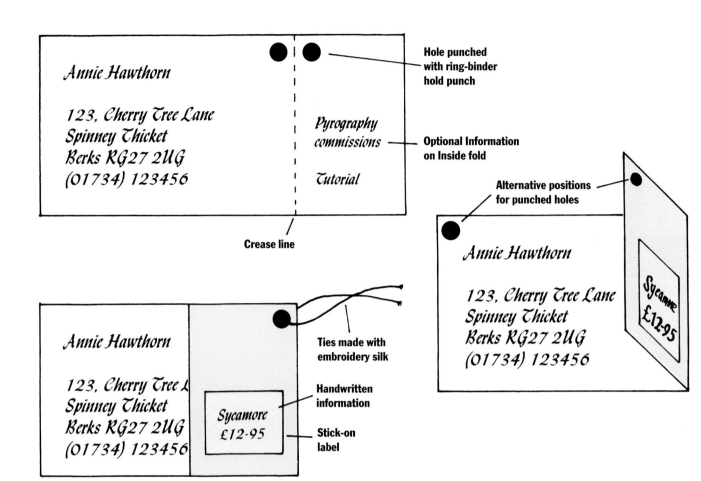

Annie Hawthorn

123, Cherry Tree Lane
Spinney Thicket
Berks RG27 2UG
(01734) 123456

Pyrography commissions

Tutorial

Hole punched with ring-binder hold punch

Optional Information on Inside fold

Crease line

Alternative positions for punched holes

Annie Hawthorn

123, Cherry Tree Lane
Spinney Thicket
Berks RG27 2UG
(01734) 123456

Sycamore £12·95

Annie Hawthorn

123, Cherry Tree L
Spinney Thicket
Berks RG27 2UG
(01734) 123456

Sycamore £12·95

Ties made with embroidery silk

Handwritten information

Stick-on label

possible for the simple reason that when they met me they were able to take a card from my display.

The early bird . . .

Make sure you arrive at the venue as early as possible. Check with the organizers the earliest time that you can get into the building. If you have constructed a display stand based on my simple plan (*see* page 135) it can be put together quickly, but you need time to organize the display of your work. I have sold quite a lot of items to other stallholders by being ready for action, and demonstrating, before the doors have been opened to the public. By arriving early, you will probably find a more convenient parking space, making unloading your gear and then packing it away again afterwards much less of a chore.

■ **What to sell**

Craft fairs are visited by a vast cross section of the public and it would be unlikely if the range of products on your display appealed to every taste. You might as well accept right away that there are some people (fortunately not many) who are never impressed by pyrography, and will not stop at your stall. However, there are many who will, and these potential customers will all be interested in different things. It is therefore worth thinking of your products in terms of how to appeal to the widest range of people.

'Cheapies'

When I first decided to try and sell my work, I went to ask a well-known local craftsman for his advice. Keith Pettit, a

Fig 16.5
The multi-use business card. It would be printed in one colour on one side. Punch your own holes and use sticky labels for the price information to keep costs down.

corn-dolly maker, has been doing the rounds locally for years, and with the combination of a smallholding and his regular appearances at craft venues, has managed to support his wife and two children. Keith is a North Essex countryman, and after carefully scrutinizing the samples of work I had brought, he said: 'What you need is "cheapies" my boy'. He was most complimentary about the work itself, but explained to me that what I needed was a range of items, the bulk of which should be inexpensive or 'cheapies'. At the time I remember arguing that in my opinion the public would be happy to spend £10 or £15 ($15 or $25) on one of my pyrographed pieces, such as cheese or breadboards. Keith's answer, backed up by years of experience, was, indeed they might, but the majority of them would be more likely to buy a wooden spoon or key-fob for £1 or £1.50 ($1.50 or $2.35), with only the occasional customer buying the more expensive and elaborate items. In other words, if you want to be sure of taking any money at all, make sure you have some cheapies. And of course, he was absolutely right.

For some examples of what might be included in this category as well as ideas for decorating them, see Chapter 17. My cheapies included items such as decorated wooden spoons, key-fobs, wooden brooches, thimbles, lightpulls, letter openers, wooden eggs, egg cups, napkin rings and bangles. All these items were priced between £1.50 and £2.50 ($2.35 – $3.90). Being small they never took up much room, either packed or displayed, and when there was only a small space for demonstrating, these were the items I used.

Middle-range items

The next area of your display that needs to be addressed is the more 'middle-of-the-road' items (*see* Figs 16.6 and 16.7). This includes the following, most of which are available as blanks from a number of outlets (*see* page 11):

- Cheeseboards
- Herb boards
- Platters
- Mug trees
- Single-rose vases
- Rolling pins
- Utensil holders
- Bowls
- Breadboards
- Memo boards
- Teapot stands
- Keyholders

Again, ideas for decorating many of the above items are featured in Chapter 17.

Fig 16.6
Single-rose vases.

These items can normally be priced at anything from £5 to £25 ($7.85–$39.20) depending on the elaborateness of the design, the cost of materials and the time spent working on it. A simple large vegetable chopping board with a small, simple design could be bought as a blank for £5 ($7.85), and sold for £10 ($15.70). However, the same board with a much more elaborate design and possibly personalized with an inscription, could be sold as a wedding present for £25 ($39.20).

A selection of these items, interspersed with the cheaper ones, would make a very interesting basic display. Make sure when you are setting it up that cheap and more expensive items are mingled together. If the first view the potential customer has of your display is of a group of rather costly looking bits and pieces, the other items may go unnoticed.

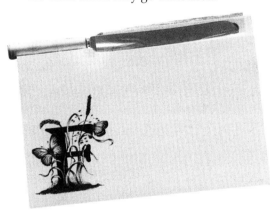

Expensive items

You may have occasionally produced pieces of work for which it is difficult to imagine how you will get a price commensurate with the effort and time put in: a framed pyrographed illustration, or a complete set of matching kitchenware for example. You will never have many of this kind of work, mainly because of the time it takes to produce them. It never hurts to have the odd expensive piece on display. For a start it will show people what you are capable of, and might induce someone to commission you for a similar piece. Also, an item on display for £250 ($392)

certainly makes a key-fob for £1.50 ($2.35) seem a bargain by comparison. Lastly, I have often heard disgruntled stallholders who have had a bad day complain that people do not wish to part with their money. I can assure you that when most people see something they really want on display, if at all possible, they will buy it, and the price will be a secondary consideration.

■ Communication

Demonstrating

Even with a well-stocked, well-lit, colourful display stall, containing a range of items priced to suit all pockets, you can still do a lot more to improve your selling chances. Unless there is no power source available (and personally I would avoid this kind of event), you must demonstrate your craft. You are displaying goods which show a lot of specialized skills, yet the vast majority of the people viewing them will not have the faintest idea how the work has been produced. To the uninitiated, pyrography can still appear at first glance to be something else.

There is no need to be seen working on a large, elaborate piece; your cheaper items are going to be sold first, so it is a good policy to be replacing them as you go. Use a small table lamp to work under with a spotlight bulb, as this will make it easier to spot you. The sort of designs that you are likely to put on the simpler items should themselves be uncomplicated and easy to execute, if necessary, while talking to someone. Do not worry – you will soon be able to do this. Producing work while at an event has other advantages. It will stop you getting bored if it is quiet, and if you are bored you may be tempted to leave your stall and have a wander. Also, if sales are a bit slow you will still be earning money in a roundabout sort of way, by keeping up production. It must always be assumed that you will sell

Fig 16.7 (left)
A breadboard.

everything you produce eventually.

Talk to people

Never be secretive about the way you work. It is unlikely that questioners are trying to prise top secret methods out of you; more likely, they are genuinely interested in you and your work, and are very likely to make a purchase. Allow those that request it to have a go on the equipment. If nothing else it will show them and anybody else watching that it is not as easy as it looks. Again, this could be all that is needed to persuade a would-be purchaser to buy something.

There is never any need to pounce on anyone who is showing interest with an ill-timed 'May I help you?'. This will put people off if they think they are being pressured. But *do* talk to people. Visitors to craft fairs seldom bite, and you can start the conversational ball rolling with just about any sane comment on just about any subject that comes to mind. Honesty is the best policy, people will appreciate and understand any comments you might make in conversation about how you have learnt your craft, and how you are supplementing your income by selling your wares.

I have often seen wonderful craftwork, exquisitely displayed on a well-organized stand, with the person responsible hiding behind it scared that somebody might speak to them, or ask a question about their work. Whatever you do, do not make the same mistake.

You will from time to time be asked questions about your work which will seem inane to say the least. For example, 'Where does the ink come from?' (an old favourite of mine); 'Do you have lots of different nibs?; and 'Do you make all the things yourself?' Be patient and explain how the equipment works. If you suggest to the person making the enquiry that they are a moron for asking such a question, you wouldn't honestly expect them to purchase from you, would you?

Even if you do not advertise the fact, sooner or later you will be asked to engrave names or some other inscription on a purchased item, and once you have been spotted doing this, 'they will all want one'. For a simple calligraphy method, *see* page 149.

Other places to sell your work

Craft fairs and village fetes are by no means the only places where you will be able to sell your work. When your work has reached a suitable standard, sooner or later a shop will show an interest, and perhaps make an enquiry regarding the retailing of your work. You should always treat such enquiries with a certain amount of caution. Most shops expect to be able to mark up goods bought in for resale by up to 100%. This means that to keep their selling price realistic they will have to buy from you more cheaply than you would be selling at one of your craft functions. Do not be tempted by the fact that, this way, you are selling a lot of items in one go. They will still have taken just as long to make.

However, a lot of shops, particularly craft shops and centres, will sell your produce for you 'on commission'. This means they will take usually between 20% and 30% of the purchase price. This I always feel is a much fairer transaction as it enables you to increase the price of your work by a relatively small amount to cover the commission you will be losing.

There are many businesses and institutions such as building societies, libraries, insurance offices and travel agents that are happy to let you display your work merely as an added attraction for their customers. I once had a display of my pyrography in the window of a travel agent in Canada for two weeks. It attracted so much interest that I was able to sell enough work to pay for my trip, and I even took some orders which I completed in the UK and then posted on.

Companies benefit from promoting crafts in this way in terms of good public relations. Similarly garden centres, especially in the winter, will often let you set up a display of work and a demonstration. They are even happier if you pay for a little advertising in the local paper to announce on which dates you will be in attendance.

If you are lucky enough to be near a camping or holiday site, you might like to try something similar with the proprietors. A camp site / garden centre at Clippesby in Norfolk was my venue for two consecutive Easter and summer school holidays: a great way to have a holiday and be paid for it.

■ Pricing your work

This is a very difficult one; there can never be any hard-and-fast rules to suit every individual's work. However, here are a few tips and comments that might help:

1 When pricing a particular piece of work, take into account your costs. These will usually comprise things like cost of materials used and time taken to produce the finished item (you will have to decide on a sensible hourly rate that you would be happy to earn for doing the work).
2 Make an allowance for what I would term, 'the degree of difficulty'. In other words, you have gone to a considerable amount of trouble to learn this particular skill; to what extent does the piece of work you are pricing reflect that skill?
3 If you are commissioned to do a special piece of work, even if the piece is to be based on something that the customer has seen on your display, extra charges must be made. You will inevitably spend more time on the job; you will probably also have to do some research to find a pictorial reference, and all this should be reflected in the price.

I used to tell prospective customers that they could have any kind of illustration on any item, and I soon realized that I was just giving myself a lot of extra and difficult work. This should never be a problem if you explain to the customer that the medium of pyrography is more suited to some subjects than others.
4 On no account *give* your work away. If sales are a bit slow, do not start reducing the prices just for the satisfaction of making a sale, however much you are tempted. People come to craft events to look at and buy items that are individually produced. Department stores and large chain stores are filled with mass-produced framed prints, and so on. If you make a purchase from any of these places, the chances are you will be buying an item identical to the thousands that fell off the same conveyor belt. Your display on the other hand comprises items made by you one at a time. The customer who takes home a piece of your work can be confident that he or she has the only one. If you have not had a good selling day, you will still have the work to sell on another occasion, so if you sell your work for anything less than it is worth, you are doubly the loser.

Once you have considered the above suggestions – and made an allowance for how much you actually admire the item and would be willing to pay for a similar piece yourself, were you offered it – you have a basis for pricing your work.

CHAPTER 17

Simple Projects to Sell

This chapter will be of primary benefit to those wishing to sell their work or, at the very least, produce inexpensive items as gifts. This may not suit those pyrographers concerned with producing the more involved pictorial pieces, nor those who wish to produce work entirely for their own gratification. Nevertheless, whatever your particular pyrography interests are, the sale of any work can contribute to the cost of prepared blanks and other materials.

If it is your aim to display work at craft fairs and venues, you will need to have a selection of the cheaper items (*see* pages 138–9). Your more elaborate and expensive pieces will no doubt sell, but a good selection of cheaper ones will sell more consistently. The way I have decorated the blanks in this chapter is not necessarily the way you will want to decorate yours; nevertheless I will describe what I have done and why, and perhaps this may provide the spark for your own inspiration.

in the kitchen for rolling biscuit pastry. They were purchased very cheaply from a kitchen reject shop and appear to be made from a beechwood. Despite their small size, they possess rather a lot of wood surface, and the temptation could be to spend a lot of time producing elaborate patterns or designs.

■ Mini rolling pins

Despite the fact that the rolling width of these items is only 4¹/₂in (114mm), I am assured that they are not produced as ornaments but are intended for use

Fig 17.1
Mini rolling pins.

Two things to remember are:

1. The receiver of this piece of work is unlikely to use it as a rolling pin, especially if a name or message has been added. More likely, it will be displayed on a shelf.
2. However much work and effort you put in, there will be a limit to what you can charge for such a piece.

The challenge with awkwardly shaped pieces such as these, is figuring out how best to work on them. The method I suggest is to build a pile of ply offcuts to a certain height so that the heel of your hand can rest on the ply and work comfortably on the pin. Your other hand can hold the handle of the pin, rotating it slowly as your design progresses across the surface. (*See* Chapter 12 for guidance on pyrographing woodturned objects.)

I have kept my designs as simple as possible. On three of the rolling pins I have allowed for an area where a message or name can be pyrographed. The gaps have been created with the help of masking tape adhered to the surface to give a line to pyrograph from, and then removed when the design has been completed. The right-hand one was decorated using Janik's G4 solid-point machine.

■ Wooden spoons

This is probably the most commonly available wooden blank of all, and can be found in a whole range of different stores and hardware retailers. It is hard to imagine a craftwork pyrography display that does not include even a few wooden spoons. Apart from the pyrography, there are a number of ways they can be utilized. They are a useful addition to the background or back of a display, drilled through the top of the handle and hung with leather thonging or ribbon.

I remember during my early craft fair days being asked many times for spoons decorated for a bride with the names of the bride and groom, date of the wedding etc. The spoon then became a part of the bridal bouquet and was carried down the aisle. Again, keep the work simple and not too time consuming. Take into account the fact that very few will be sold as they appear on the display; names and details will probably have to be added. I have worked on the convex area of the spoon, but there is no special reason why one cannot pyrograph the other side. However, you will find the spoon more rigid placed flat side down on your work table and therefore easier to work on. Whey you are buying your spoons, examine each one carefully and only pick the best ones. They are normally made from a beechwood, but if well sanded with some medium-grade sandpaper, they give a smooth surface to work on.

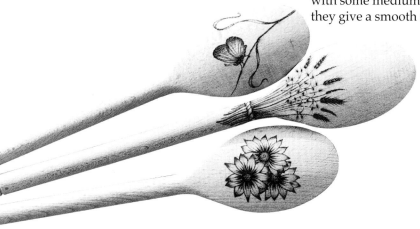

Fig 17.2
Wooden spoons.

Fig 17.3
Matching brooch and earrings.

■ Earrings and brooches

These are fun to do and can be an opportunity to introduce a flash of colour to a display. The earring blanks are ash and the brooch blanks are sycamore. Both are from Janik, and even with clip and pin fittings are only a few pence to buy. Such small pieces of wood are of course difficult to work on (the earrings are only one inch in diameter). If you stick a small piece of Blu-tack to the underside of each piece, they can be attached to a strip of birch-faced plywood, several at a time if need be, enabling you to work on them as you would a flat surface. Try not to leave the Blu-tack on the wood for too long, however; it contains an oil which, if allowed to soak into the wood, can impair the strength of the glue used to attach the fittings.

If seen displayed away from any other pyrography it would be difficult to detect the use of pyrography on these earrings and brooches, particularly the matching red and black set (*see* Fig 17.3). I used the Janik G4 solid point to produce these items, and ordinary designers' gouache for colouring them. Using a small sable brush you will need to apply two to three coats of the colour to give it density. Sometimes a precise little engraving with just a hint of colour, as in the case of the fish (*see* Fig 17.4), will give a display of small items such as these the contrast that makes them more interesting.

The final protection, always needed where a little water-based colour has been added, comes with the application of a very thin transparent lacquer. One coat on a brooch will dry in a couple of minutes. Ordinary varnish, by contrast, tends to fill in some of the detailed texture (e.g. the fins and scales of the fish), and takes a long time to dry. If you require a matt finish, one or two coats is all that is needed; for a more glossy finish just build up further coats. The glue used to attach the clips and pins can be any contact or multi-bond adhesive suitable for gluing a porous to a non-porous surface. To aid adhesion I recommend scratching the metal surface of the fitting and the wood surface to which it is to be adhered with a sharp point prior to gluing.

Fig 17.4
Earrings.

Fig 17.5
A brooch.

◼ Key-rings and key holders

These are another knick-knack must, almost on a par with the famous wooden spoons. Blanks can be obtained very reasonably and in a good range of different shapes. These are the sorts of items that can be produced quickly and easily – ideal for a display on a cork noticeboard, and an ideal project to be working on while demonstrating at a craft fair. It is always a good idea to have a selection of things that can be displayed by hanging. The pieces shown in Figs 17.7 and 17.8 were all produced using the Janik G4 solid point.

Rectangular and other-shaped plaques can easily be made into key holders (*see*

◼ Small framed pictures

I have been producing these for a number of years now for my pyrography displays, and pride myself on the attention I give them. Subjects such as the butterfly (*see* Fig 17.6) actually take a considerable time to complete because of the attention to detail. A lot of care has to be taken working at slow speeds and low temperatures. The border around the illustrations has been created by placing masking tape round the outer edge of the ply, which is then removed after the pyrograph has been completed. I have dispensed with an overlay mount.

As well as being very rewarding to do, they are cheap in terms of materials. The frames measure 4 x 4in (102 x 102mm) square and contain a birch-faced plywood offcut approximately 3^1/$_2$ x 3^1/$_2$in (89 x 89mm) square. Providing you are prepared to buy a sensible quantity, most picture framers will be happy to make you some of these small frames from offcuts of a length that would normally be scrapped.

The amount of money that these minor works of art can be sold for, especially if they are in sets of three or four, justifies the time that is spent on them. The illustrated offcut and glass are simply held in position by two layers of masking tape; a single brass eyelet for hanging is incorporated with the tape.

Fig 17.6
A set of small framed pictures.

Fig 17.8). Try to vary the designs of both key-rings and key holders as much as possible if you are going to display a number of them. I once made 24 identical key-rings with a blackberry motif, and arranged them on a cork noticeboard. People must have assumed that I had attempted to mass produce, and it was a very long time before any of them were sold.

◼ Jotter boards

This is a slightly more expensive item to buy as a blank, although they would be

Fig 17.7
Key-rings.

Fig 17.8
A key holder with matching
key rings.

Fig 17.9
A jotter board.

easy enough to make yourself with a few
simple tools. One advantage with them is
that, after allowing for the space taken up
by the note pad, there remains only a
small area to place a design, thus
discouraging the temptation to produce
an elaborate piece of pyrography.

tendency is rather to proudly display it.
With any display there should also be
similar items that can be used without
fear of spoiling the design. This board has
been decorated around the edge with a
simple repeat leaf pattern with provision
for an inscription at the top and bottom.

■ Round breadboards

This type of breadboard is available from
any number of reject and hardware shops
around the country. The surface on the
one in Fig 17.10 was not particularly good
for any detailed work, being made from
several joined pieces of very hard beech.
Sometimes, as in the case of a particularly
detailed design on an expensive board of,
say, English sycamore, commissioned
perhaps as a wedding gift, there is a
reluctance to actually use it, and the

Fig 17.10 (right)
A round breadboard.

Fig 17.11
Cheese platters.

Cheese platters

This is another inexpensive buy from the reject shop. These items represent a compromise between the elaborate and expensive pieces in the 'special gifts' category, and the cheaper items which can be either for actual use in the kitchen, or for hanging up on the wall. I have pyrographed a simple design on each one in the bottom left-hand corner (*see* Fig 17.11). A message or a couple of names can be easily added to turn these into personalized gifts, and there will still be plenty of room for the cheese.

Sycamore breadboards

This breadboard (*see* Fig 17.12) with its magnetically attached stainless-steel knife probably represents a slightly higher class of item than many of those featured in

this chapter. The board is beautifully made and the design applied to it will have taken some time to arrange on the wood and pyrograph. Nevertheless, whatever its eventual price, its presence in a display will lend more credibility to the prices of the cheaper items on offer.

Fig 17.12
A sycamore breadboard.

Fig 17.13
Always practise on a spare piece of wood before executing an inscription.

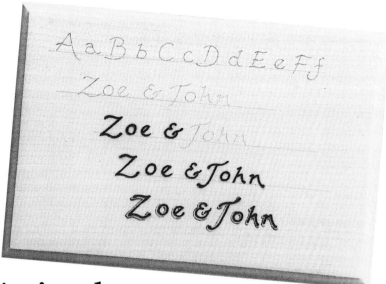

A simple calligraphy method

My own method of pyrographing inscriptions evolved from requests at craft shows by purchasers of my work. I soon learnt that I simply could not afford the time to make a meal of it. Often attending these fairs on my own, I had to come up with a way of doing this job quickly to avoid missing the next potential customer. This was my method:

1. Devise a simple alphabet that can be drawn carefully onto the wood – freehand if possible.
2. Encourage the customer to keep the inscription as brief as possible.
3. Write the letters in pencil on a ruled line, slightly overspacing them (*see* Fig 17.13). If you are nervous about working with a soft pencil directly onto the wood, you can get round this by attaching a piece of greaseproof paper with masking tape to the surface of the wood and working from the tracing once you are happy about the positioning.
4. Set the wire point to a reasonably low temperature to enable you to make the darkest and deepest possible mark; you will have to work very slowly to do this. As always, a practice run on a scrap of wood is advisable.
5. Once the letters have been completed, use the soft rubber to remove any visible pencil marks.
6. Carefully bend the point towards you by pressing it against a piece of scrap wood in the reverse of the direction in which you have been pyrographing. When you turn the pyrography pencil back to its normal position, you will be working with the top of the end of the point, which will enable you to produce a much finer line.
7. Turning the temperature down significantly in order to produce a fainter line, pyrograph a shadow line to each letter, being careful to ensure that the spacing stays as constant as possible.

Of course you can go to much greater lengths than this, but this simple method is really all you need when people are waiting to have a name or brief inscription pyrographed, and with a little practice it can be done very quickly and accurately.

Index

About the Author

Stephen Poole was born in Buckinghamshire in 1948. The son of a maths teacher, he was rapidly frightened off numbers and opted for a more creative direction at the Windsor Grammar School – where he will be remembered for a near perfect, prize-winning soprano voice – and Berkshire College of Art where he did a three-year course in graphic design.

Since 1975, Stephen has spent his time developing his own particular pyrography techniques, latterly running courses to pass on his adopted craft to others. This book, based on the course, has been written by popular request, as there is no other practical and comprehensive guide to pyrography in existence.

TITLES AVAILABLE FROM GMC PUBLICATIONS

BOOKS

WOODWORKING

Beginning Picture Marquetry	*Lawrence Threadgold*
Carcass Furniture	*GMC Publications*
Celtic Carved Lovespoons: 30 Patterns	*Sharon Littley & Clive Griffin*
Celtic Woodcraft	*Glenda Bennett*
Celtic Woodworking Projects	*Glenda Bennett*
Complete Woodfinishing (Revised Edition)	*Ian Hosker*
David Charlesworth's Furniture-Making Techniques	
	David Charlesworth
David Charlesworth's Furniture-Making Techniques – Volume 2	
	David Charlesworth
Furniture Projects with the Router	*Kevin Ley*
Furniture Restoration (Practical Crafts)	*Kevin Jan Bonner*
Furniture Restoration: A Professional at Work	*John Lloyd*
Furniture Workshop	*Kevin Ley*
Green Woodwork	*Mike Abbott*
History of Furniture: Ancient to 1900	*Michael Huntley*
Intarsia: 30 Patterns for the Scrollsaw	*John Everett*
Making Heirloom Boxes	*Peter Lloyd*
Making Screw Threads in Wood	*Fred Holder*

Making Woodwork Aids and Devices	*Robert Wearing*
Mastering the Router	*Ron Fox*
Pine Furniture Projects for the Home	*Dave Mackenzie*
Router Magic: Jigs, Fixtures and Tricks to	
Unleash your Router's Full Potential	*Bill Hylton*
Router Projects for the Home	*GMC Publications*
Router Tips & Techniques	*Robert Wearing*
Routing: A Workshop Handbook	*Anthony Bailey*
Routing for Beginners (Revised and Expanded Edition)	*Anthony Bailey*
Stickmaking: A Complete Course	*Andrew Jones & Clive George*
Stickmaking Handbook	*Andrew Jones & Clive George*
Storage Projects for the Router	*GMC Publications*
Success with Sharpening	*Ralph Laughton*
Veneering: A Complete Course	*Ian Hosker*
Veneering Handbook	*Ian Hosker*
Wood: Identification & Use	*Terry Porter*
Woodworking Techniques and Projects	*Anthony Bailey*
Woodworking with the Router: Professional	
Router Techniques any Woodworker can Use	*Bill Hylton & Fred Matlack*

WOODTURNING

Bowl Turning Techniques Masterclass	*Tony Boase*
Chris Child's Projects for Woodturners	*Chris Child*
Decorating Turned Wood: The Maker's Eye	*Liz & Michael O'Donnell*
Green Woodwork	*Mike Abbott*
A Guide to Work-Holding on the Lathe	*Fred Holder*
Keith Rowley's Woodturning Projects	*Keith Rowley*
Making Screw Threads in Wood	*Fred Holder*
Segmented Turning: A Complete Guide	*Ron Hampton*
Turned Boxes: 50 Designs	*Chris Stott*
Turning Green Wood	*Michael O'Donnell*

Turning Pens and Pencils	*Kip Christensen & Rex Burningham*
Wood for Woodturners	*Mark Baker*
Woodturning: Forms and Materials	*John Hunnex*
Woodturning: A Foundation Course (New Edition)	*Keith Rowley*
Woodturning: A Fresh Approach	*Robert Chapman*
Woodturning: An Individual Approach	*Dave Regester*
Woodturning: A Source Book of Shapes	*John Hunnex*
Woodturning Masterclass	*Tony Boase*
Woodturning Projects: A Workshop Guide to Shapes	*Mark Baker*

WOODCARVING

Beginning Woodcarving	*GMC Publications*
Carving Architectural Detail in Wood: The Classical Tradition	*Frederick Wilbur*
Carving Birds & Beasts	*GMC Publications*
Carving Classical Styles in Wood	*Frederick Wilbur*
Carving the Human Figure: Studies in Wood and Stone	*Dick Onians*
Carving Nature: Wildlife Studies in Wood	*Frank Fox-Wilson*
Celtic Carved Lovespoons: 30 Patterns	*Sharon Littley & Clive Griffin*
Decorative Woodcarving (New Edition)	*Jeremy Williams*

Elements of Woodcarving	*Chris Pye*
Figure Carving in Wood: Human and Animal Forms	*Sara Wilkinson*
Lettercarving in Wood: A Practical Course	*Chris Pye*
Relief Carving in Wood: A Practical Introduction	*Chris Pye*
Woodcarving for Beginners	*GMC Publications*
Woodcarving Made Easy	*Cynthia Rogers*
Woodcarving Tools, Materials & Equipment (New Edition in 2 vols.)	*Chris Pye*

VIDEOS

Drop-in and Pinstuffed Seats	*David James*
Stuffover Upholstery	*David James*
Elliptical Turning	*David Springett*
Woodturning Wizardry	*David Springett*
Turning Between Centres: The Basics	*Dennis White*
Turning Bowls	*Dennis White*
Boxes, Goblets and Screw Threads	*Dennis White*
Novelties and Projects	*Dennis White*
Classic Profiles	*Dennis White*

Twists and Advanced Turning	*Dennis White*
Sharpening the Professional Way	*Jim Kingshott*
Sharpening Turning & Carving Tools	*Jim Kingshott*
Bowl Turning	*John Jordan*
Hollow Turning	*John Jordan*
Woodturning: A Foundation Course	*Keith Rowley*
Carving a Figure: The Female Form	*Ray Gonzalez*
The Router: A Beginner's Guide	*Alan Goodsell*
The Scroll Saw: A Beginner's Guide	*John Burke*

MAGAZINES

WOODTURNING ◆ WOODCARVING ◆ FURNITURE & CABINETMAKING ◆ THE ROUTER
NEW WOODWORKING ◆ THE DOLLS' HOUSE MAGAZINE
OUTDOOR PHOTOGRAPHY ◆ BLACK & WHITE PHOTOGRAPHY
KNITTING ◆ GUILD NEWS

The above represents only a selection of all titles currently published or scheduled to be published. All are available direct from the Publishers
or through bookshops, newsagents and specialist retailers. To place an order, or to obtain a complete catalogue, contact:

GMC Publications,
Castle Place, 166 High Street, Lewes, East Sussex BN7 1XU United Kingdom
Tel: 01273 488005   Fax: 01273 402866   Website: www.gmcbooks.com   E-mail: pubs@thegmcgroup.com
Orders by credit card are accepted